BORN
ON
THE BATTLEFIELD
TRINITY

BORN
ON
THE BATTLEFIELD
TRINITY

A Thorn in the Flesh

JOHN HENRY JAMES 3RD

authorHOUSE®

AuthorHouse™
1663 Liberty Drive
Bloomington, IN 47403
www.authorhouse.com
Phone: 1 (800) 839-8640

Published by AuthorHouse 03/10/2015

ISBN: 978-1-4969-7308-5 (sc)
ISBN: 978-1-4969-7307-8 (e)

Print information available on the last page.

Any people depicted in stock imagery provided by Thinkstock are models, and such images are being used for illustrative purposes only. Certain stock imagery © Thinkstock.

This book is printed on acid-free paper.

Scripture quotations marked KJV are from the Holy Bible, King James Version (Authorized Version). First published in 1611. Quoted from the KJV Classic Reference Bible, Copyright © 1983 by The Zondervan Corporation.

Contents

For:
Tammy L. James, Nelijah R. James,
Monique E. James, & Tamara A. James

Foreword

Well Dear Reader, we are embarking on yet another journey into, as yet, uncharted territory. Prayerfully I have been able to charter **some** of it for you in the two previous Born on the Battlefield books *The Art of Spiritual Warfare* and *The Reality of Spiritual Warfare?*

We see in scripture, that The Apostle Paul had a 'thorn' in the flesh. We are not told what that thorn was in the physical. What we *are* told is that it was a messenger of Satan that was assigned to him to trouble him and beat him up on a regular basis. We have to understand that God's plans and ideas don't necessarily include *or* incorporate our plans and ideas. Our ideas, aspirations and plans have to be according to His will. His will, however, always works out to *our* benefit; if we *stand*!

This book will speak to you about today's world and Jesus' return to earth. It will speak to you about how the enemy is stepping up his attack, in these last days, and the importance **right now** of God's people securing and holding onto their faith. It will impress upon you the vitality of using the <u>art</u> of spiritual warfare and convince you to recognize the reality of what is going on; both **<u>on</u>** and **<u>behind</u>** the scenes.

Hold on Dear Reader; we are about to take one Heaven of a ride!

Let's dive right into the water with both feet.

All Hell is breaking loose and the general population does not seem to be paying attention. From my standpoint, things changed in the spiritual and in the natural on September 11, 2001. Not to say that this was *the* event that changed the world, but 911 was definitely a landmark to surpass any other landmark in history. Far too many of the world's hopes, dreams, aspirations and confidences revolved around America being a 'heaven on earth'. It was the apex for opportunities; the land of the free and the home of the brave. America was the country that the world aspired to be like and that everyone wanted to get too. America was the place where dreams came true! My apologies Dear Reader, but that all disappeared on 911! Maybe not as literal as I am making it sound, but literally in the sense that 911 made the world stand up and take notice. America was catapult into becoming a police state.

The entire world has been trying to place things back into perspective since then, but as we press forward, into the future, the reality of the world before 911 seems to be getting further and further away. The stock market may go up and then go back down; jobs may seem to appear for a while and then disappear; people may carry on with their daily routines, but the secure relaxed feeling, that was once the 'American *Dream*' disappeared on 911. People do not feel safe anymore and it is because Satan has injected fear into the world in a very big way.

The world was already heading in the wrong direction; 911 just solidified this for everyone who was 'not' paying attention. Not that I have come up with something new or something that had never been heard of or done before, but the frequency and depth of what is happening post 911, as well as the *way* that it is happening, is surreal.

People are not afraid to challenge morality, justice, integrity, the status quo or just the plain difference between right and wrong. They have all jumped ship and many people have lapsed into a mentally, self absorbed state of thinking. Today everything is allowable, acceptable, and permissible as long as people in society can justify it in their *own* minds.

The thinking nowadays is that anything that I do sexually is okay, as long as my partner consents; doesn't find out about it; or if others are in agreement with me. What I choose to do or wear in public is the next step in 'trendsetting' and the 'right wing' should loosen up. If my behavior is offensive, then please feel free to turn your head or turn the channel. Do not bother me and I will try not to bother you! Everyone, or so it seems, is doing what they think is right in their own eyes.

Well Dear Reader, everything is **NOT** okay!

My children always hate when I tell them what the older generation always tells them, *"When I was your age..."* I understand that and I suppose all young people go through that stage in their lives. What happened and did not happen when I was their age, however, is a reality. News reporters on television used to cry on camera when people were killed especially children. People were shocked and appalled when crime hit their neighborhood and they collectively took a stand against it. It was never the 'norm' for a missing child to have the parents as the ones responsible for their disappearance or to have parents as irresponsible as they have become today. This was not how life was a very short time ago.

Having a night out with the person you loved did not require one to be on the constant lookout for what was lurking in the shadows. Adults were expected to carry themselves in a certain way and not mimic or try to impress their children or their children's friends. *They* were the adults after all. What was heard over the airways and reported in the newspapers was something that did not make a person uncomfortable on a daily basis. Courtesy was common and having simple compassion for your fellow man was viewed as something normal rather than the 'norm' becoming to turn a blind eye to the misfortunes of others. This was not how life was a very short time ago.

People going to their house of worship for service or bible study, during the week, was common on certain days and seeing people enjoying themselves at a park or fair ground did not require so great a police presence. People watched one another's homes and property for anything suspicious and the neighbors could leave town without being apprehensive about what they would find upon their return. Women were not used to being referred to in a negative fashion and young men still wore their clothing the way that they were supposed too. Using foul language spoke about your character and upbringing and what *you* thought about who *you* were. Having too much skin showing told everyone that your self esteem was low or that you were actually trying to attract a certain type of attention or both. This was not how life was a very short time ago.

A 'social network' used to be a group of people that got together and tried to better themselves and their communities. The world did not dictate how people *thought*; how they *responded* to one another. They did not dictate what *was* or *was not* acceptable behavior or what would be the next thing that they would or would not be interested in. People used to be real with themselves, their situations and the world around them. They did not mysteriously transform into *their* fantasy vision of themselves in 'cyberspace'. A hard working person would give you their best each and every time they were to execute their job, duty, or the required task at hand. Most people took pride and respect in whom they were and gladly showed the entire world, instead of wanting to imitate whoever was popular. When we start to look at and begin to see what has and still is being pumped into our brains; how depraved our thinking has gotten; and how Satan is molding us into his image and likeness, it's going to hurt! This was not how life was a very short time ago. Not at all!

How did we get from the 'Leave it to Beaver' and 'Father Knows Best' remember these (if you are old enough to remember these shows) to 'Desperate Housewives' and 'Sex in the City' era in less than fifty years? How did we get from "*He's the pastor of that church...*" to "*He has children by all of these women at that church.*"? What happened to the time when the older men and women were examples of what the younger men and women wanted to grow up to be? Who said that it was okay to wear a shirt where your favorite football team mascot had its middle finger up cursing the opposing team or to publicize cartoons or cartoon characters urinating on the logo of the team that was their rival? When did cartoons need a separate channel or special timing for adult content like 'adult swim'?

I cannot be the only person in the world that remembers how different things were not as long as say a hundred years ago, or fifty, or twenty, or even ten years ago. Take a moment and think! Who have we become? Who are we becoming? Is it so difficult for us to think for ourselves today; for us to mentally go back to a time that was, to put it simply, a clearly better way to live? We have been deceived and the worst part of it is that we like it. Everything has become a '*high*' to us; everything tickles our flesh and feels good to us. Everything caters to what is making an odor rise in the nostrils of God that He will have to assuage and stop. I can not be the only one that can see this; not the only voice of one crying in the wilderness?

How can we hope that things will get better when we don't give credit and honor to the one who can make it better?

I have asked you, Dear Reader, to think about and to answer a lot of questions. However, I have done my part in placing you in remembrance of the direction that we *ought* to walk so the accountability is now yours. If we are claiming to hold up the banner of Christ and we have somehow missed the mark; we have to ask ourselves honestly, *"What direction are we really going in?"* *"In what direction do we want to go?"* *"Where do we hope to end up?"* *What is my purpose and am I fulfilling it?"* Remember this, *"Above all else; know thyself!"*

The path is not always clear; it is not always easy to locate; it has not always been walked beforehand. Sometimes we have to be game-changers; trailblazers! Sometimes we have to forge a way so that others can follow in our footsteps. When we make it over the wall, we have to throw back a rope so that others can *follow.* We must never build the wall higher.

> *"And lest I should be exalted above measure through the abundance of the revelations, there was given to me a thorn in the flesh, the messenger of Satan to buffet me, lest I should be exalted above measure."*

> 2 Corinthians 12:7

> *"Are you the barbed wire trying to choke the rose or are you the rose pressing to grow through the wire?"*

God's Job

Like a Good Father

"According to the word that I covenanted with you when <u>ye came out of Egypt</u>, so my spirit remaineth among you: <u>fear ye not</u>."

Haggai 2:5

When the Father of everything that is and of everything that will be; tells us not to fear, why do we still fear? It is because we do not *trust*. I listened to a sermon; given by Elder Francisco West at New Vision for Life Church; and he spoke about this very same issue. If God has defeated your enemies and has shown you things that no one else has ever seen; if He has shown *you* the impossible; if He has proven His power time and time again; why would we not think that *He* would get frustrated with us? He does, He did and He is. The Israelites were saved because Moses dared to intervene with God's plan. Moses, however, did exactly what God wanted Him to do; He *reasoned* with God and made sense.

"And the LORD said unto Moses, I have seen this people, and, behold, it [is] a stiffnecked people: Now therefore let me alone, that my wrath may wax hot against them, and that I may consume them: and I will make of thee a great nation."

"And Moses besought the LORD his God, and said, LORD, why doth thy wrath wax hot against thy people, which thou hast brought forth out of the land of Egypt with great power, and with a mighty hand? Wherefore should the Egyptians speak, and say, for mischief did he bring them out, to slay them in the mountains, and to consume them from the face of the earth? Turn from thy fierce wrath, and repent of this

*evil against thy people. **Remember Abraham, Isaac, and Israel, thy servants, to whom thou swarest by thine own self, and sadist unto them, I will multiply your seed as the stars of heaven, and all this land that I have spoken of will I give unto your seed, and they shall inherit [it] for ever."***

*And the **LORD** repented of the evil which he thought to do unto his people.*

Exodus 32:9-**14**

Moses reminded God that they were *His* people and that *He* was the one that freed them. He also reminded God of *His* promise to Abraham, Isaac and Jacob/Israel. He reminded God that *He* swore by *Himself.* So God changed His mind.

God's job is to prove us to His enemies and to ours. He is like any other Father, He wants us to succeed and do well. He alone wants the bragging rights when that day comes. He will then be able to tell Satan, Satan's whole army, and every angel in heaven and not in heaven, *"**Look at my child!" "He/She did well huh?**"* This is the righteousness of God and His justification. It justifies and solidifies His Word *and* our testing.

Sometimes we will take more time than we ought to and go through more than He wants us too, simply because we do not trust our Father. His job is like any Fathers job; to watch over, teach and protect.

His testing comes in a variety of ways and is for a variety of different reasons. For some things, he will give us Godly grace. Some things He has given us in His Word. Other things He allows us to see through the experiences of life and through others. It may seem like He is holding us too close at times, but this is because He knows better. At other times, He will give us the freedom to experience certain things in life for ourselves. If our tests go right, then we have done well. If they go wrong, He expects us to confide in and come back to Him so that we can receive further instruction.

God created man so that He could express His love in a different way. He has never entered into this type of a relationship with any of His other creation. God has created the universe and set His angels in place to insure that all things are operating within His will and to perform the duties for which they were created however we are not slaves or robots. We also have free will. We see this in the fact that Lucifer rebelled and took one third of the angels with him. This is proof that they have the free will to be disobedient and to choose, like any other conscious created being.

A practice of those who use oxen to plow farmland is to take a mature, well seasoned, trained ox and yoke it to a younger ox so that it can be taught. The younger ox will become accustomed to the gate and the direction, which the older ox is going, and will learn. The older ox teaches the younger ox to be obedient, to move in unison with him and to accomplish the given task with less trouble. This is why Jesus tells us to take *His* yoke upon us and learn from *Him*. He tells us that His yoke is easy and His burden is light and that we can find rest in Him for our souls. Jesus wants to be yoked with us, not for restraint, but for teaching us and to show us the way.

Understanding this; makes it easier to grasp the fact that we are to ask God that His will be done. It makes it easier for us to understand that our burdens do not have to be as hard as we make them. Our burdens become harder only when we want to plow the field the way that *we* see fit; it makes us want to buck against the one driving the oxen and pull away from the one that we are supposed to be yoked too. Notice that I did not say that we would not have any burdens? We will have burdens to bear, but Jesus is telling us that they can be made easier.

> *"Take **my yoke** upon you, and **learn of me**; for I am meek and lowly in heart: and ye shall find rest unto your souls. For **my yoke [is] easy**, and **my burden is light**."*

> Matthew 11:29, **30**

So God's job, if we can call it a job, is to be God! He certainly knows what He is doing; why He is doing it; and what His plans are. We are His children who keep asking, *"Are we there yet?"* We need to be obedient and sit still. If the road takes a turn, we must stay in our seats and remain confident in the fact that He knows the road and how to get us to where He is taking us. I am certain that, while His path may be foreign to *us*, it is much better than our Father allowing us to ride with strangers.

Notes And Reflections For The Reader:

Notes And Reflections For The Reader:

Satan's Job –
Don Lucifero

(Perversion)

I say Don Lucifero because Lucifer is trying to play God's people like he is some sort of Godfather and his word is law like he is a mafia boss. He has the fallen angels and God's people convinced that he is making offers that cannot be refused. The fact of the matter is that they *can* be refused and that is exactly what God wants us to do.

> *"Submit yourselves therefore to God. Resist the devil, and he will flee from you."*

> James 4:7

Satan cannot make us any offer that we cannot refuse. We must take a step back; look at who's making the offer; what the offer is, and what is the fine print. The fine print with Satan and with God is always your life in exchange for accepting that offer. Upon finding out that the offer is from Satan, then we stop right there. The payoff, at the end of the day is eternity; will you spend it with the Don or will you spend it with the King?

Don's have a reputation for being very cruel when their orders are not followed to the letter. Even with those that have a notable name and rank in their 'crew'; they tend to be very brutal and malicious, in order to send a message and make an example for those that would not follow. Our Father's offer is much more promising.

Satan's job is very simple and it does not change. The only parts of his plan that change have to do with the situation and circumstances. The main plan does *not* change. The plan is to steal, kill and destroy always! If he cannot steal it directly from you, then he will trick you into forfeiting your possessions or get someone else to trick you and/or steal it from you. If Satan cannot kill you, then he will petition God to allow him to make you wish that you were dead. He will always use everything in his arsenal to destroy everything that God has blessed you with. He wants to destroy God's purpose in your life. He will attack your ministry, your purpose and anything that may save, encourage or assist someone else in their ministry or purpose. Anything that might promote the word of God and His gospel.

He does this by using the same three methods every single time: the lust of the *eye*, the lust for the *flesh* and the *pride* of life. It is really that simple; no new tricks; no new plan; no grandiose mathematical calculation. All of sin falls into these three categories all of the time; Satan just rehashes them to make them fit *his* agenda.

If Satan can get us to a point where he makes us doubt God then he has succeeded in a portion of his plan up front. Once we take our eyes off of the only person that can turn us around and point us back in the right direction, then we become lost in the woods and make God's job, as a Father, more difficult.

Satan's bottom line is to **pervert** God's creation!

PERVERT
per·vert [*v.* per-vurt; *n.* pur-vert]

1. to affect with perversion.
2. to lead astray morally.
3. to turn away from the right course.
4. to lead into mental error or false judgment.
5. to turn to an improper use; misapply.

EXPAND
noun

10. a person who practices sexual perversion.
11. *Pathology.* A person affected with perversion.

12. person who has been perverted, especially to a religious belief
regarded as erroneous.

Satan wants to do all of the above with God's creation. Number five
is the definition that I use most often to describe perversion. When
something is designed for a certain purpose and is being used for a
completely *different* purpose, then it is being perverted.

If I use a shoe to bang a nail into the wall, then I <u>can</u> *force* it to work,
but the shoe was never designed to drive nails. I can use a screwdriver
to pry open a paint-can lid, but the screwdriver would be being
misused. This is what Satan seeks to do with our gifts and talents.
Think about how many people have grown up in the house of God;
gotten their training and talent in church and then find out that they
can make so much more money if they use their talent for the world.
It takes a persuaded mentality to make the correct decision when the
enemy dangles the world in our faces.

When we see the newest pop-stars [lyricists], song writers, musicians,
comedians, actors, etc…we should read their bios on the internet
and see where they are from and where they got their training and
inspiration. You would be surprised that many of them them started
in church.

At some point Satan will want to collect on his contract. This shows
up in our lives after Satan has stolen our youth and our credibility. If
we know the Hip Hop rappers, that were the first ones to jump start
the industry, they are probably around my age now or a little older,
late forties (43) very few of them were able to transition into different
venues in order to continue their lifestyle. What has amazed me is
that many of them are claiming to be prophets, priests, reverends
and the like and now, what used to be a musical genre is now being
called a religion! Certain moguls in the rap industry are beginning
to outwardly practice Satanism, witchcraft, Wicca, and the rights
of free masonry and the Illuminati (the enlightened ones). To know
that these things exist in the world and that there are adults that
have chosen these different paths is a matter of common knowledge
or simple research. To have Satan take a further step and want to

inject these idealisms into our children is an indication that nothing is sacred any longer. The gloves have been taken off. I am bothered by the fact that the people making the most money; selling the most music and that have become the most influential in today's society are the ones that are reaching out and trying to take hold of our children.

We truly have to watch and pray and view ourselves as '*watchmen on the wall*' when it comes to our progeny. Satan is attempting to pervert and use for his purposes, the gifts and talents of generations to come before they can even recognize that this is a war.

When we see pre-teens in third-world countries carrying automatic weapons and that know how to act as members of a military unit, while still at the age where they should be in grade school, they have been brainwashed and used. This is what Satan wishes to do with any young person that has potential; any young person that can be a potential asset to the 'Kingdom's' side. If we remember Nebuchadnezzar in the book of Daniel, who came and stole all of the best and brightest that Israel had and used them for his purposes, we get an idea of what Satan is trying to do.

> *"And the king spake unto Ashpenaz the master of his eunuchs, that he should bring [certain] of the children of Israel, and of the king's seed, and of the princes; <u>Children in whom [was] no blemish, but <u>well favoured</u>, and <u>skillful in all wisdom</u>, and <u>cunning in knowledge</u>, and <u>understanding science</u>, and <u>such as [had] ability in them</u> to stand in the king's palace, and whom they might teach the learning and the tongue of the Chaldeans."*

Daniel 1:3-**4**

Think about it; we are seeing younger and younger children stepping into areas that were commonly considered places and roles that could only be filled by adults. It is becoming common place to see thirteen or fourteen year olds open a concert for well known 'idols.' These 'idols' are sending a secular message to the world at large. Children are now targets for getting adult messages into society. Children are the targets of the newest and latest technological advances and are the catalysts for making breakthroughs unlike the world has ever known. Children have become the leaders in how company's market, advertise, promote and make their money. In sports, fashion, music, food, entertainment and almost everyplace else where money can be made, there is a venue to draw the young.

If you doubt what I am writing:

Mark Elliot Zuckerberg *(born May 14, 1984) is an American* computer programmer *and* Internet entrepreneur. *He is best known for co-creating the* social networking site Facebook, *of which he is* chief executive *and* president. *It was co-founded as a private company in 2004 by Zuckerberg and classmates* Dustin Moskovitz, Eduardo Saverin, *and* Chris Hughes *while they were students at* Harvard University. *In 2010, Zuckerberg was named* Time *magazine's* Person of the Year. *As of 2011, his personal wealth was estimated to be **$17.5 billion**.*

I do not have the time to list all of the negative aspects that have come through FaceBook, but the target market is children. Children barely old enough to have a computer now have a FaceBook page as well as the older generation who have been sucked into it. Almost everyone that does have a computer now has a FaceBook, Twitter, or like pages, but the youth are the target of these industries. The youngest person that I know of is seven and the oldest is seventy-three. The damage of this newest craze has been listed on the internet, with more frightening tales being broadcast daily.

FaceBook and like technology, if utilized correctly, could be the *single* most effective evangelistic tool on the planet. Instead it has become one of the *single* most silently destructive tools of the enemy in history without a bomb ever having to be dropped. Marriages have been destroyed, people have ended up in prison, houses have been burned to the ground, pedophiles have used this as a way to satisfy their appetites and people have even lost their lives all because of this indiscriminate 'social network'. Quite frankly, people are losing their hold on reality in 'cyberspace'.

It has all come about at the hands of a young man that was barely in his twenties when the idea entered his mind and, if I am staying true to form in my writing, he is an Israelite. He is one of the best and the brightest (intelligent); he was well favored (attending one of the best colleges); skillful in all wisdom (computer technology and computer language); understanding science (computer programming) and had the ability to stand in the king's palace ($17.5 billion in his twenties made him the youngest billionaire on earth).

Isn't this what Nebuchadnezzar wanted with Israel's children? To teach them what he wanted them to learn; to teach them his language for his own purposes? If you cannot understand what I am trying to communicate Dear Reader, you must at least see that the similarities are far too great to be ignored. As I have stated countless times before, "The greatest trick of Satan is convincing the world that he does not exist!" FaceBook caters to the lust of the eyes, the lust of the flesh and the pride of life in every way imaginable. Like David says, *"Selah or think about that."*

Whether you believe these things or not, Satan has found a way to pervert what essentially should be among man's greatest achievements in this the twenty-first century. I have a FaceBook page and it is used to minister the gospel of Jesus Christ, win souls, and minister to those who desire it. If I am being transparent; I can see the allure and how people get sucked into wanting to make this a part of their daily routines and it is alluring! What can be done with this tool; and that is truly all it is, a tool; has never been able to be done prior. I am able to keep contacts with pastors that I met in Africa almost ten years ago and they have no electricity to speak of. They may live in the jungle and use firelight to see their way around at night, but if they walk far enough to a place that will allow the use of the internet, they all have a FaceBook pages. That was amazing to me in a way that I can hardly describe on these pages.

> *"And this gospel of the kingdom shall be preached in <u>all</u> the world for a witness unto all nations; and then shall the end come."*

> Matthew 24:14

The capability is here and the gospel *will* be preached in all the world very shortly, if it has not already been. We can see why Don Lucifero is calling his crew in to put in extra work. It's like the Feds have him in their sites and he needs to get his top earners to get as much as they can before his *family* gets sent to prison. (Forgive me; I am speaking in terms of how the 'mafia' operates so that you get a clear picture)

Satan will pervert as much of God's creation as he can before his time comes. That is his only way he feels as if he can get back at God. I know what the Word of God says, but God has not shown *all* of His cards yet! God has something more unexpected than we can ever imagine in store for Satan and his followers. Before all is said and done, we will be able to see why the angels in heaven praise him day and night!

Notes And Reflections For The Reader:

Notes And Reflections For The Reader:

Our Past Defines Us

We Are Products of Our Past?

"That which hath been is now; and that which is to be hath already been; and God requireth that which is past."

Ecclesiastes 3:15

We may not want to face this fact or even admit it to ourselves, but the truth is the truth is the truth. I grew up a certain way and that's how I expected my life to be when I was grown. It is only when a person places God into the equation that they will ever be able to break free of the chains of their past; no matter how comfortable those chains have become. In this scripture Solomon is actually saying that God requires our past so that He can make us a 'new' person in Christ Jesus. A better way to say it is that He requires that we give it to Him. He doesn't want us holding onto things that have previously held us down. He doesn't want us to remain in bondage when we can be free. He wants our mind bodies and souls free from our pasts so that when He places a new spirit within us we will be 'Kingdom' ready. Keep in mind that the best or worst part of eternity is that our minds do not change or die. Getting a 'Kingdom' mindset needs to be accomplished now!

I plan to have better things to think about when I get to God's 'Kingdom' than the fact that I am free from everything that bound me here on earth. I want to have more to praise God for than the fact that my earthly chains are broken. I don't want to spend my eternity thanking God for what I can thank Him for now, but that is reason enough! God might say, *"John I heard you, but get to work doing your **new** heavenly job."* God is real and we have to think about Him that way.

Therefore if any man [be] in Christ, [he is] a new creature:_ old things are passed away; behold, all things are become new.

2 Corinthian 5:17

"Know ye not that we shall judge angels? How much more things that pertain to this life?"

1 Corinthians 6:3

"And hath made us kings and priests unto God and his Father; to him [be] glory and dominion for ever and ever. Amen."

Revelation 1:6

How can I become a judge if I am weighed down with the baggage of my past? It would be very difficult to judge angels in eternity if I have not gotten rid of my earthly issues. In that same regard, how could I become a king or a priest? Kings must be level headed at all times and able to make 'Kingdom' decisions. Priests must be able to carry out their priestly duties in a way that others will be able to rely on them and trust that they have the ability to go before God on their behalf.

If my past is to define me, then I want it to define me from the standpoint of having a 'Kingdom' mindset. Too many people in today's society are controlled and bound by their pasts. It has become a business to keep people tied down by the things that they should have been loosed from as a matter of normal maturation. Don't get me wrong, tragedy is definitely more difficult to deal with than poor parenting, but when you can identify the problem, you have already begun to make progress. Knowledge still is power!

Too many in today's society are bound by entitlement issues where they have adopted the mentality that because they did not receive the best of everything when they were a child, they deserve all of the bells and whistles in their adult life. No! Everyone does not get everything in life that everyone else gets. My apologies Dear Reader, but those are just the rules. If one child got a pony when they were ten years old and you still want one at forty years old, then you need to work, save your money and plan on how you can get a pony. Maybe you would take into consideration that since you did not get a pony at ten and since your are forty now, you can substitute the pony for a mustang?

Now victims of molestation, rape or abuse need counseling and more in depth intervention. It is, however, possible to move past these issues in life and become and obtain everything that God has purposed for you. Take some time and do the research on the background stories of people that have had these kinds of traumatic experiences in childhood and turned their stumbling blocks into stepping stones. If I hear one more person cry or complain about something that has happened to them forty years ago; that they have not dealt with or tried to rectify it head on as a rational adult; you will hear me scream through the pages of this book! At some point in life we must stop being the victim and take _ownership_ of our own lives. If you had it bad growing up, what are you going to do about it? **You** are still alive and **you** still have an opportunity to turn things around for **yourself**.

We can be products of our past or we can choose not to be. My Father died from leukemia when I was one year old. He saw me before he passed and that gives me a great deal of comfort. On the other hand, I grew up seeing other young men's father's come to school; come to our football games; support them in life and there was always that empty space inside of me. At a certain point in my life, I began to realize that I wasn't the only one that had been affected by the death of John H. James Jr. My mother was pregnant with my younger sister Tracey when he passed and from the time I was born, all I've ever heard was how much I looked and reminded everyone of him. [Thanks to Margo and BarbaraJean Ellis for remembering Johnnyboy] At a young age I stopped asking my mother questions realizing that it was a painful memory. So what did I do? I took ownership and decided that, if he was not around, then I would be everything that I would have wanted him to be in my life so that I could be a good father and a good husband to my wife and children. Simply put I wanted to be what I've heard about him. I listened to the older men who had successfully raised children and had endured in marriage. I selected good role models and made mental files of the things that my elders were teaching me. No one ever told me that anything was going to be easy, but I made up my mind early in life that I would not become a victim of my past. Why not turn my liability into an asset? If not for myself then I would do it for my wife and children? *Hurt* people *hurt* people and this realization was on the extreme opposite of the spectrum from where I wanted to go in life.

We have to make certain decisions early on in life before we get to a point where we have simply wasted too much time! We have to look at our life in terms of one very simple fact; we only get one! Let's not waste any opportunities and let's not spin our wheels doing nothing while we have time and chances. The funny thing about the past is that it does exist, but that's why they call it the past. You cannot live there while you are in the present!

Notes And Reflections For The Reader:

Notes And Reflections For The Reader:

Our Present is Relevant

This is a Lifestyle; a
Way of Living

"Then Peter said, Lo, we have left <u>all</u>, and followed thee. And He said unto them, Verily I say unto you, There is no man that hath left house, or parents, or brethren, or wife, or children, for the kingdom of God's sake, Who shall not receive manifold more <u>in this present time</u>, and in the world to come life everlasting."

Luke 18:28-**30**

The experiences that we go through and the decisions that we make in life create and tell a story about who we are. If *something* happened to us and it was good and we handled it with humility, modesty and reserve, then that can tell a certain story about us. If *something* happened to us and it was bad and we handled it by being: deceitful, vicious, vindictive and malicious, then that tells a different story about us.

This speaks to whether or not we have character and integrity or the lack thereof. It tells people of our disposition and temperament. It also can determine what types of friends and associates that we will have; who we will include in our 'circle'; who we will associate with or distance ourselves from; and who will or will not be drawn to us.

God allows what He allows for His glory and for the glory of the Kingdom. It may not feel good to us, but it is for *His* purpose and ultimately for *our* benefit. We must learn to look at the circumstances in our life as the way that God sanctifies and purifies us. His goal is to ready us for the mindset that we will need to have for when we get to the 'Kingdom'. If we are led down a path that teaches us humility, then it is because God desires that it be a character trait of 'Kingdom' citizens. If we are led down a path that breeds patience, then it is another quality that will be required in heaven. If we are led down a path of longsuffering, then it is yet another trait that will prepare us for our heavenly duty. We will have the titles of *Kings* and *Priests* when we get to heaven; so the traits necessary to fulfill these duties are being instilled in us now! The same two scriptures apply to our present life.

> *Know ye not that we shall judge angels? How much more things that pertain to this life?*

> 1 Corinthians 6:3

> *And hast made us unto our God kings and priests: and we shall reign on the earth.*

> Revelation 5:10

If we look at this scripture then we can see why God allows us to undergo some of the things that we must endure while here on earth. We must learn to look at things from a heavenly perspective so that we are not discouraged. If we are unable to grasp what God's Word tells us while we are here on earth, then we might give up the battle before we reach the mark of the *'high calling'* of God. We must be contenders for the faith and know what God's word says.

> *"And <u>hath raised [us] up together</u>, and made [us] sit together in heavenly [places] in Christ Jesus..."*

> Ephesians 2:6

> *To the intent that now unto the principalities and powers in heavenly [places] might be known by the church the manifold wisdom of God...*

> Ephesians 3:10

It's a now thing. We have to realize that we are to be living a power filled, God glorifying, world changing, life, right now! When the enemies of God see us, they should see us seated in those heavenly places. I've heard that message before in church and it never really rang truly clear. Look at it this way. When demons, principalities, powers, the rulers of darkness, and even sinners see us, they should see something different. They should see us clothed in the uniform of an ambassador from our Kingdom. Our citizenship should be recognized and we should command from everyone the respect for our King and our Country.

We shall give an account of what we have done with the training that we have had while here on earth. This is what goes into helping us to fulfill our purpose or we will lead a life where our purpose is never fulfilled.

The first topic that I always teach a new class is *purpose*. If I can get someone to understand that God has a purpose for their life, then half of the work of teaching is done. If a person understands that God has given them a purpose; that He has designated a purpose for them for a reason, then a thirst for learning is developed and cultivated. Treasure begins to be sought and learning begins to take place outside of the classroom.

Tragedy strikes when we begin to look at the tests that God places before us as 'too hard' or 'not attainable'. On the contrary, He will test us according to what He seeks from and for our lives and according to what we've studied and know about His Word. God will *never* tempt us, even though we are tempted in like fashion as was Christ, but rather He will not allow the enemy to tempt us beyond what we can handle or are able turn away from.

> *"There hath no temptation taken you but such as is common to man: but <u>God [is] faithful</u>, who will not suffer you to be tempted above that ye are able; but will with the temptation also make a way to escape, <u>that ye may be able to bear [it]</u>."*

> 1 Corinthians 10:13

Let no man say when he is tempted, I am tempted of God: for God cannot be tempted with evil, neither tempteth he any man:

James 1:13

What the enemy does is take what he knows about us and uses it against us! Character flaws, personality traits, likes and dislikes, etc... These small things allow him to manipulate us and set 'booby traps' in our path during the course of our lives. Why do you think that God's word is so necessary? He is omniscient and He knows what we are going to experience during the course of our lives and what the enemy will attempt to do to derail us. This, by no means. negates free will and we do *always* have choices. Those choices we make let God know whether we are learning the lessons that He is teaching us. Those choices also allow the enemy to strategize against us. It is a scary thought to recognize that we must continually fight an unseen enemy that is older than time, stronger than us, and bent on destroying everything that God has designed and planned for our lives; God's purpose in us. This is why Jesus came! We use *Christ's* power; *Christ's* righteousness; *Christ's* justification; *Christ's* grace and mercy to counter the enemy's attacks and show Satan defeated in our lives and for those that look to us as examples.

This is why our present defines us as much as our past. Everything that goes into making us who we are is relevant. Our heritage is relevant, our society and the culture we live in are relevant, our parenting is relevant, our relationships are relevant, and so much more. When we take as much of this into consideration as possible, we can begin to fathom the intricacy of spiritual warfare.

When we also factor in that we are confined to time, then we can further conclude that these things are being examined by God and plotted against us by Satan from the moment of our conception. The things in our past also determine our present character. Our character consists of who we are as well as who we would like to be and how we are shaped and are shaping the course of our lives. Who we would like to be takes work. The things that shape our lives are, for the most

25

part, the things that God allows and we must also take into account, with some regard, time and chance.

"I returned, and saw under the sun, that the race [is] not to the swift, nor the battle to the strong, neither yet bread to the wise, nor yet riches to men of understanding, nor yet favour to men of skill; but <u>time</u> and <u>chance</u> happeneth to them all."

Ecclesiastes 9:11

We are all a product of time and chance. It does not seem spiritual does it? Look at it this way; God gives us time like money. We can spend time wisely or waste it. We can use it to grow or abuse our use of it and remain stagnant. If we use our time wisely, we grow. Then we can consider ourselves productive. If we abuse it then we risk not meeting the purpose for which God has designed us. We are to be patient and hold our peace like Isaiah and God will allow us to move when he will.

O LORD, be gracious unto us; we have <u>waited</u> for thee: be thou their arm every morning, our salvation also in the time of trouble

Isaiah 33:2.

<u>I have long time holden my peace</u>; I have been still, and <u>refrained</u> myself: now will I cry like a travailing woman; I will destroy and devour at once.

Isaiah 42:14

Chance simply speaks to those events in our lives that remind us of the fact that we live on a planet that is teaming with plant and animal life; a planet that has weather patterns and is effected by the part of the universe in which it exists. We also are surrounded by other types of earthly life that we have no control over and have yet to discover. Chance is simply God's world in operation.

It was chance that killed so many in the Indonesian Tsunami, in the New Orleans Hurricane, in the Japanese Tsunami and in the Haitian and Venezuelan Earthquakes. It was by chance if you were someone that happened to live in these areas when the disasters struck home. It was by chance that the people that died did not live in places where they could have been survivors of the same tragedy. Since *time* and *chance* happen to every man, is it not wise to prepare for the place where we will spend eternity before placing our fate in the hands of either one or allowing the enemy to lead us?

> *For with the heart man believeth unto righteousness; and with the mouth confession is made unto salvation.*

> **Romans 10:10**

We will then have a greater opportunity to understand that we are not the make of our own destiny, *if* we would simply heed the warning signs of the experiences that we have in life; *if* we learn from the experiences of others; *if* we have wise elders that will point us in the right direction at an early age. If we have parents that live like hell and throw caution to the wind; never caring about anything beyond what is immediate; living like there are no consequences to their actions; parents and elders that draw close to God with what they say, but their hearts are not with God, then we will be in trouble. This means that then, we will have less of an opportunity to look at eternity from an objective standpoint.

Let me dispel this myth. I have often heard the question, *"What if someone lives in a place where they never get the opportunity to hear the message of Jesus Christ?"* No excuse! My answer is that if someone never gets the opportunity to hear about our risen Savior then God will judge that person on whether they have recognized Him and His work.

> *"For the invisible things of him from the creation of the world are clearly seen, being understood by the things that are made, [even] His eternal power and Godhead; so that they are without excuse:"*

> Romans 1:20

This scripture clearly tells us that what we cannot see in the spiritual realm is clearly seen by what God has created in the temporal realm. In other words, *"there had to be a watch maker if there is a watch"*. Things just don't happen in an ordered fashion. In fact, it has been scientifically proven that order deteriorates over time; order spirals into chaos rather than progresses toward perfection. In science this is called The 'Chaos Theory'.

If the *past* didn't define us, and we are confined to time and space, then how would we learn, grow and progress from even the simplest things that have been learned or discovered; the things that aid us in our daily lives? If the past and *present* were irrelevant then how would we cope with the curves that are thrown at us by the world on a constant basis? How could we make present decisions that would impact or help determine a positive future? Man is so focused on his future now that he cannot learn from his past the way that God spells it out in His word.

For those persons that do not receive the 'good news' of our Savior the Word says:

> **"But if our gospel be hid, it is hid to _them that are lost_:"**

2 Corinthians 4:3

Notes And Reflections For The Reader:

Notes And Reflections For The Reader:

I Have No Man

Are You Self-Sufficient or God-Sufficient?

"The <u>impotent man</u> answered him, Sir, I have no man, when the water is troubled, to put me into the pool: but while I am coming, another steppeth down before me."

John 5:7

When you get to this point in life, it is usually a turning point. It is the point at which you have an epiphany; a moment of clarity, if you will? It is the point in your life when God forces you to realize that, in order to take another step in life, you have to turn your focus toward Him and *keep* it there. It is the point where you have nothing; do not have anything to lose and have no one to turn too. It is the point in life where *you* have become the impotent man!

I reached that point where I was used to relying on myself and relying upon what I knew to get me through life. I was saved and relying on God's grace to provide my daily bread, to bless me with work, to lead my family and for the flow of my ministry, but I wasn't giving God 100%. Imagine how distraught I was when God said that it was not enough.

God: *How are you John? We are not as close as we once were.*
John: Hey *Dad!* I'm cool and doing everything I know to do and it is all working out well!
God: That's the problem. Soon you'll begin to believe that it's all in your power.
John: My family is fine, my business is fine, my ministry is fine, my health is fine…what else do I need to do Lord?
God: Be willing to let it all go.

31

John: I am willing Lord.

God: Why do you keep calling me Lord and don't do **exactly** what I say?

John: You are the Lord.

God: No John, *you* are Lord.

John: Why do you say that Dad?

God: I thought we were going somewhere *together* John?

John: We are! I'm sitting right beside you. Why wouldn't we be going somewhere together?

God: Because you are still trying to drive.

John: I'm not trying to drive, I was only giving directions.

God: Then take your hands OFF of the steering wheel!

Well, He showed me; the same way that He showed Job.

That was the first book in scripture that came to my mind when my walls started to crumble. One of the first prayers that I prayed was, *"God I will not curse you or turn my back on the faith."*

I believe that *this* mentality and my confession of faith to God and myself stopped me from giving up. I believe that it saved me from dying. What do you do when one of your children is removed from your home? What do you do when your wife turns her back on the faith and follows after the world? What do you do when the respect that you once had is turned to shame and you become a laughing stock? What do you do when you lose the use of your body and can no longer perform the most menial of tasks like write your name, take a shower on your own, or button your shirt? What do you do when you lose everything that you've worked for? What do you do when your faith is shaken to the core?

You have to *know* that you *know* that you *know* in your **knower** that God is still on the throne and that He is in charge and driving! If you do not, then you will have a very short shelf life. It becomes a matter of time and then the enemy will begin to tear down every part of your life that still has meaning. It becomes 'down hill' and often times it turns out to be very difficult to get off of the roller-coaster.

And the Lord said, Simon, Simon, behold, Satan hath desired [to have] you, that he may sift [you] as wheat:

Luke 22:31

I came to that point in my life in 2008, but realized that it all began in 2004. Satan desired to sift me like wheat and I just was not paying attention. He always desired to destroy me, but the hard part about that was trying to understand that *someone* or *something* was trying to kill me and knowing also that you've done nothing to deserve it except *exist*.

But when Jesus knew it, he withdrew himself from thence: and great multitudes followed him, and he healed them all;

Matthew 12:15

"The impotent man answered him, Sir, I have no man, when the water is troubled, to put me into the pool: but while I am coming, another steppeth down before me"

John 5:7

[Let me say this about the troubling of the water. You may not agree with my analogy, but I ask you to please continue Dear Reader and please feel free to let me know if you disagree. I believe that Satan was troubling the water at the pool of Bethesda. Doesn't Satan want God's place? Can't Satan perform miracles? Isn't Satan the God of this world for now?

For Jesus to supersede something that God was doing with the water in the pool of Bethesda would mean that He acted on His own; apart from the trinity. If God had arranged a set time and season for people to get healed and in a certain way for their healing, then Jesus would have been totally wrong to heal the man at the pool. The scripture only tells us of an angel that troubled the water at the pool. It does not say whose team the angel was on. It does not indicate that this was an act of God like the serpent on the rod in Exodus that was established for healing. Please note that in Matthew 12:15 Jesus healed them *all*!]

"And the LORD said unto Moses, Make thee a fiery serpent, and set it upon a pole: and it shall come to pass, that every one that is bitten, when he looketh upon it, shall live."

Numbers 21:8

God healed *everyone* that believed enough to look on the fiery serpent.

My point is only that God takes credit and gets the glory for what He does. That element is not present here in this story; only the assumption, but I believe a correct one. God does get the glory in the form of Jesus.

Why do I make a point of the man by the pool? He was asked a simple question, that Jesus already knew the answer too, "Do you want to be healed?" It seems like a question that should have been obvious, but it was also a testing of the man's faith. I believe that Jesus was looking around the pool and was saying to Himself, *"I am right here!"* *"Why are you waiting on the water to be troubled?"*

When the impotent man said I have no help, Jesus told him to get up. Not only did the man get up after being in that state for thirty-eight years, he picked up his bed and walked away with new strength in his legs.

When we are faced with situations in life; *God* will send our help so that our attention and focus remain on Him. He does not want us to rely on man; only to recognize that He and He alone has sent our help. That man would have never forgotten the person that set him in the pool. As it turns out, he never forgot Jesus and he arose immediately.

And immediately the man was made whole, and took up his bed, and walked: and on the same day was the sabbath.

John 5:9

34

We also tend to forget that we are the clay and God is the potter. We continue to look to other pieces of clay for help and guidance and forget that they are also pieces of clay. We cannot rework ourselves, so it stands to reason, that other clay vessels are in no position to help us. We cannot remove our own imperfections; we cannot reshape ourselves into the image that will benefit the potter; only the potter knows what He needs. Only the potter knows what He wants to use us to accomplish.

When we have problems in life, we have been programmed by society to seek assistance from our families, friends, co-workers, talk show hosts, etc. and we usually end up with more questions than answers. It is always an exercise in futility when we do not ask God, pray, and wait for His reply. Sometimes we must stifle ourselves and listen instead of consistently talking. Our problem, most often, ends up taking us back to the fact that we are that child in the back seat repeatedly asking, *"Are we there yet?"* In other words, the problem is *impatience*!

God's Word tells us that *tribulation* works patience in us. Did we think that God can not rework us on His potter's wheel from where He is? Life *is* the potter's wheel! [I minister to never ever pray for patience because then we are asking for more tribulations.]

> *"And not only [so], but we glory in tribulations also: knowing that <u>tribulation worketh patience</u>; And <u>patience, experience; and experience, hope</u>: And <u>hope maketh not ashamed</u>; because the love of God is shed abroad in our hearts by the Holy Ghost which is given unto us. For when we were yet without strength, in due time Christ died for the ungodly. For scarcely for a righteous man will one die: yet peradventure for a good man some would even dare to die. But God commendeth his love toward us, in that, while we were yet sinners, Christ died for us."*
>
> Romans 5:3

Paul is telling us in Romans, that our trials and tests are God's way of giving us *patience*. From learning how to be patient we are gaining *experience* and once we have that, our hope is increased. We may have an initial hope, but we will gain a **bold** hope through knowing that god is ever present and cares about our situation. Through gaining this bold hope we become unashamed of the gospel and are able to minister in a *new* way with *new* confidence.

A large part of the type of vessels that God creates, is up too *us*; whether we are to be vessels of *honor* or *dishonor*. What determines this is how pliable we are in the potter's hands. If we continue to resist the potter's handiwork and make it difficult for Him to work with us, then it will take Him longer to get us shaped into the vessel that He wants us to be. If we prove to be continually difficult, then we could end on the pile of broken pieces that the potter has determined is not worthy to continue to be worked with. Pliability allows us to be shaped into whatever He needs at whatever time He needs us.

When we get to the point in life where we realize that we have no man, it is actually at that point, that God wants us to recognize that our focus is not on Him. The man was able to turn his focus away from his problem long enough to talk to Jesus. God is stimulating us to pay attention and realize that our focus is in the wrong place and on the wrong things. We will try to search out a man to help us through our situation, but there will be no man. We will look for a group or proposed expert to help us deal with our situation, but to no avail. We will try what has always worked for us in the past, but *that* will no longer work. It will be when we recognize that God has allowed our situation, for His glory, that we will begin to understand. It is at that point that we will begin to feel God drawing us closer. It is at that point that we can be shaped and molded; it comes when we have become broken and are completely malleable.

The realization that the potter is the only one that can remove our defects; shape us and mold us; turn us into something that no one ever thought was possible for us to be; is the first step in our becoming what will be a vessel that He can use. It is when we are honest enough with ourselves that we can say, "Okay, we have no man." We have abandoned hope of getting into the pool under our own steam. It is when we have abandoned the hope of the help we depended on that will get us to our healing. We have reconciled within ourselves that there is nothing for us to do save be still. This is when God will come along and make sure that our faith is strong enough for us to stand up on our own feet; pick up our beds and walk away from our situation *immediately.*

We will find new strength, new hope, new energy, and have greater faith than we had before. We will be able to tell the story of how we lay in our broken state for thirty-eight years and then God sent Jesus to do the impossible. We will be able to say that it was not the troubled water or the help of a man that instituted our healing, but the one that God sent. We will proclaim the gospel of Jesus to every other broken and marred piece of clay, and point them in the direction of the potter.

Notes And Reflections For The Reader:

Notes And Reflections For The Reader:

The World View

Microwave Thinking

(I want it now; I need it now – gimme, gimme, gimme!)

This is definitely a 'New Age' thought process.

God's way is that if a man does not work he does not eat. What are we to do with the new mentality that because someone wants something, they feel like they have the 'right' to and are entitled to have it no matter who gets hurt in the process? 'Things' get chased because of a thought of *entitlement*. It is not only children that have this mentality, but adults have adopted it as well

My belief is that this is happening worldwide, but predominantly in America. People are taking a new approach today; that they are 'owed' something; working hard to get ahead in life and get the things you want out of life has disappeared. Today, people think that they can go through life and attain, achieve, or progress having very little to account for on their part.

What has gotten people to this point? A number of things have planted this type of mentality into people's minds. The industry of professional sports has paid athletes more money than they could possibly spend in a lifetime. The DOT.com era has turned people's ideas into million dollar industries with the advent of the internet and computer technology. The music industry has turned people that cannot even sing, into celebrities that are sought after and worshiped worldwide. It has turned them into Divas which in Italian is Goddess or into 'idols' which God says we should never have or worship. Let us not get into all of the foolishness that is broadcast over the television and or movie airways in the form of talk shows, comedy, sexually alluring sitcoms and simply random garbage.

Turn ye not unto idols, nor make to yourselves molten gods: I am the LORD your God.

Leviticus 19:4

And what agreement hath the temple of God with idols? for ye are the temple of the living God; as God hath said, I will dwell in them, and walk in them; and I will be their God, and they shall be my people.

2 Corinthians 6:16

To make a point, Seinfeld was a very funny show and probably one of the most popular and longest running shows on television. Admittedly, by the show's star and the producers, the show was about 'nothing'.

This is the point that we have come too in this world; where we will eat up and tune into *'nothing'* regularly. How is this possible? We have run out of ideas that will feed our minds and allow us and those ideas to grow. When you can come up with a show about 'nothing' and become a millionaire, then where is the incentive to work hard to make an honest living?

The reason that this chapter is called 'microwave thinking' is because people inherently have no more patience.

"But thou, O Daniel, shut up the words, and seal the book, [even] to the time of the end: <u>many shall run to and fro, and knowledge shall be increased.</u>"

Daniel 12:4

"That we [henceforth] <u>be no more children</u>, tossed to and fro, and carried about with every wind of doctrine, by the sleight of men, [and] cunning craftiness, whereby they lie in wait to deceive;"

Ephesians 4:14

41

It is very easy to see that today people will follow the next thing that seems good or sounds good to their flesh. Any person that seems to have an answer to what we are going through can create a following. There is a market for every problem in today's world. In the book of Ephesians, Paul calls it the *sleight* or trickery of men that wait to deceive. These are days when everyone is deceiving everyone to line their pockets to get ahead in life or both. The newest and the latest doctrine rules the day. If Oprah says it, that is how it must be. If Dr. Phil or Maury Povich says it, then that's how we should handle our lives. Common sense and thinking for ourselves is gone! The ability to rationalize and make decisions that do not require someone else's opinion has faded into non-existence.

> *LORD, what is man, that thou takest <u>knowledge</u> of him! or the son of man, that thou makest account of him!*
>
> **Psalms 144:3**

> *O the depth of the riches both of the wisdom and <u>knowledge</u> of God! how unsearchable are his judgments, and his ways past finding out!*
>
> **Romans 11:33**

> *But grow in grace, and in the <u>knowledge</u> of our Lord and Savior Jesus Christ. To him be glory both now and for ever. Amen.*
>
> **2 Peter 3:18**

God wants us to grow in grace and in knowledge as Paul tells us in Romans and Peter tells us in 2 Peter. The book of Daniel tells us that in the last days many shall run here and there and knowledge will be increased. Look at how fast things are moving every day and how everyone is in a hurry. In a hurry to do what? Technology is definitely increasing exponentially and it will *not* stop! As fast as man can think of the next place that technology can go, it is outdated.

When one thing hits the marketplace, its replacement is already on the blueprint table.

> *"Many shall be purified, and <u>made white</u>, and <u>tried</u>; but the wicked shall do wickedly: and none of the wicked shall understand; but <u>the wise shall understand.</u>*

Daniel 12:10

The reason that Christianity is having such a difficult time today is because the ears of those that are wicked have been sealed. The wicked will not understand the simplicity of the gospel; what is happening according to God's time table; and how close we are. That is a very hard pill for them to swallow. We, as the righteous of God, are begging and pleading for the world to listen to our message so that they can escape the certain judgment and God's wrath, on that final day, but they do not understand! That is indeed a truly scary place to be. This reminds me of the book of Exodus when it says that God hardened Pharaoh's heart! God did not make Pharaoh wicked, He only allowed what was in him to come out. This is how things are *right* now. God is allowing what is in the hearts of man to come forth; it is one way to separate the wheat from the tares. It is thrown into the air together with the chaff. The wheat is heavier and falls to the ground while the chaff is lighter and does not fall the same way. It is then cast into the fire. Sounds familiar doesn't it? The wicked today are *"Tossed to and fro with every wind of doctrine…"* This is the age where two will be in the field and one will be taken; two will be at the mill grinding, and one will be taken…

> *"Then shall two be in the field; <u>the one shall be taken, and the other left</u>."*

Matthew 24:40

> *"Two [women shall be] grinding at the mill; <u>the one shall be taken, and the other left</u>."*

Matthew 24:41

> *"I tell you, in that night there shall be two [men] in one bed; <u>the one shall be taken, and the other shall be left.</u>"*

Luke 17:34

> *"Two [women] shall be grinding together; <u>the one shall be taken, and the other left</u>."*

Luke 17:35

> *"Two [men] shall be in the field; <u>the one shall be taken, and the other left</u>."*

Luke 17:36

The idea is that both were together, supposedly, doing the same work, but only one had the pretense of laboring *with* the other. One was chosen and the other was left behind. Everyone that thinks that they will make it into the 'Kingdom' is going to be sadly mistaken when that day comes. They will think to remind God of their works and He will say to them depart; you and I never had a ***relationship***.

This again is a result of 'microwave thinking'; let's get this cooked and done right now. The old way of putting something in the oven and letting it cook slowly has become outdated. The microwave way cuts out the ***'love'*** part of cooking. The presentation has disappeared; the plating is gone; the fine china and silverware have turned into plastic knives, forks and styrofoam (again this is not a gospel of works). You may still be able to stomach what is produced, but is it really good for you? How long can you eat microwave food before your body rejects it? We can eat it, but ultimately this is not a healthy continuous way to proceed and it will eventually make you sick. It is the same way with this type of thinking. If we do not earn the things that we get in life, then we place no value in them. It is like scripture says, "… *casting pearls before swine.*"

"All things are lawful unto me, but all things are not expedient: all things are lawful for me, but I will not be brought under the power of any."

1 Corinthians 6:12

We see the 'liberty' that we have in Christianity; in this scripture, but the point is that we have to be smart about how we use our liberty in Christ. It's like the younger generation that is so eager to grow up and spread their wings. They must be told that the liberties that they have earned are just that, 'earned', and that they will not be taken away unless they are *misused.*

We have the ability and freedom to do a lot more than we generally acknowledge in Christendom, but everything that we are allowed to do is not *good* for us. Those things that we are **_not_** allowed to do are clearly listed; so we do have our directions. Paul says that he will not be brought under the control of anything; he belongs to Christ!

The 'prodigal son' had this type of thinking. He had the, *"Give me mine now!"* ie. *'Microwave mentality'.* He had no patience and the lure of the world proved to be greater than he anticipated. He wanted his inheritance right then and right there; he did not want to wait. His father gave him what he wanted and not too long afterward the enemy had stolen it from him. No more money, inheritance gone, and the only thing that he had left, was the memory of what he used to have; the memory of the way he could and should have been living.

His father had some amount of wealth. His father had servants; his father had cattle, and yet the prodigal son found himself sleeping with the pigs and eating their food to stay alive. It was only after having this epiphany that he was able to move past his 'microwave thinking'. Imagine him laying with the pigs and saying to himself, *"I micro-waved the whole thing!" "I micro-waved what should have lasted me years; I could have created a place for myself in this world and now it's gone!" "I'm a Jew eating corn husks and slop! The servants eat better than this at my father's house!"*

45

It definitely takes God's wake up call to break this type of mentality. Satan has deceived the world into adopting his mindset. Pay attention when you hear people speaking about what they did not have and what they should have or could have had; and listen to them pointing out what others have. That mentality is running rampant today and what does it all go back too, the lust of the eye, the lust of the flesh and the pride of life. The same three tricks just reconstituted to fit a 2014 world.

I apologize, but when there is love and attentiveness to a well cooked meal it shines through in the food. A slow nickel is far better appreciated than a fast buck every single time because you have made earning that nickel personal. Microwave Thinking will yield no profit; it will not plan for tomorrow; it will not sustain you; and, in the end, you will always be in a retrospective position where your *current* state is far worse than your present state.

Notes And Reflections For The Reader:

Notes And Reflections For The Reader:

Notes And Reflections For The Reader:

Sunshine or Rain

I can see clearly now
the reign is gone…

"[There is] therefore now __no__ condemnation to them which are in Christ Jesus, who walk not after the flesh, but after the Spirit."

Romans 8:1

We all have a choice! It is *our* choices and decisions that draw us closer to God or pull us further away from Him. The presence of sin in our lives is described in scripture as an unpleasant odor in God's nostrils. *Injustice* is also considered to be sin in the eyes of a *righteous* God. The angels that are stationed on earth and report back to God, report this sin as a 'cry' or 'crying out'. That part of our being, that is God in us, is always uncomfortable with sin unless we sear it out of our *conscience* or harden our hearts to His still, small voice.

"And he said, What hast thou done? the voice of thy brother's blood __crieth__ unto me from the ground."

Genesis 4:10

"Speaking lies in hypocrisy; __having their conscience seared with a hot iron__;"

1Timothy 4:2

"And it came to pass in process of time, that the king of Egypt died: and the children of Israel sighed by reason of

the bondage, and they <u>cried</u>, and their <u>cry</u> came up unto God <u>by reason of the bondage.</u>"

Exodus 2:23

Abel was to be in the bloodline of Christ, but Satan slew him thinking to stop God's promise of a Messiah. God avenged Abel by excommunicating Cain and setting a mark on his forehead. I think that it was shaped like the Tree of Life, but that is my opinion. Even though God allowed the children of Israel to be taken into bondage, the injustice, of the slavery of His people, caused God to move on their behalf. Israel is considered to be God's wife in the same way that the church is considered to be the bride of Christ. How compassionate must God have been to bear witness to Satan's mishandling of His bride? How painful was it for God to watch Pharaoh kill every firstborn child of Israel in search of the Savior? Israel's cry was heard in heaven because of the sin that was visited on His people. God hears the cries of the earth whether good or bad.

And Pharaoh charged all his people, saying, Every son that is born ye shall cast into the river, and every daughter ye shall save alive.

Exodus 1:22

Sidenote: This may be why God turned the water into blood as one of the plagues against Egypt.

"And the LORD said, because the <u>cry</u> of Sodom and Gomorrah is great, and because their sin is very grievous;"

Genesis 18:20

For we will destroy this place, because the <u>cry</u> of them is waxen great before the face of the LORD; and the LORD hath sent us to destroy it.

Genesis 19:13

It wasn't the people of Sodom and Gomorrah that were crying out to God, but rather their sin which was so repugnant to God's nostrils. It caused God to send His angels to the two cities to bear witness and report. It wasn't that God could not see what was going on from heaven, but rather so that the testimony of the angels would come into account upon Judgment Day. If we remember the 'reality' of spiritual warfare, there is a certain *legality* involved in all of this. In order to be righteous in judgment, there must be witnesses to the injustice so that the defense will have no case against the prosecution. When the people of Sodom and Gomorrah stand at the White Thrown, there will be nothing for them to say. It will have been the *cry* of their own sin that convicts them.

The law was not given to man to hold him hostage or enslave him, but rather to point out our necessity for a Savior. God knows the weaknesses of man better than we know our own weaknesses. The law is a barrier that has been set into place to prevent us from running off of the road and so that we can stay focused on the destination ahead. Too often we view the law in the wrong way and are offended by it when we should really look at God's Law as street signs on the highway to eternity.

> *"For what the law could not do, in that it was weak through the flesh, God sending his own Son in the likeness of sinful flesh, and for sin, condemned sin in the flesh :"*

> Romans 8:3

Peter is pointing out *why* the law was 'weak' and could not keep man on the road to eternity. It would be like asking the street signs to drive us to our relative's house; they are simply the signs that point the way. The law was weak through the flesh because the flesh has been programmed with Satan's GPS system. God ordered us to keep all of the law or we would not see eternity.

> *Then said the LORD unto Moses, Behold, I will rain bread from heaven for you; and the people shall go out and gather*

52

a certain rate every day, that I may prove them, <u>whether</u> <u>they will walk in my law, or no.</u>

Exodus 16:4

These are the <u>statutes</u> and <u>judgments</u> and <u>laws</u>, which the LORD made between him and the children of Israel in mount Sinai by the hand of Moses.

Leviticus 26:46

And said, If thou wilt diligently hearken to the voice of the LORD thy God, and wilt do that which is right in his sight, and wilt give ear to his commandments, and keep <u>all his</u> <u>statutes</u>, I will put none of these diseases upon thee, <u>which</u> <u>I have brought upon the Egyptians</u>: for I am the LORD that healeth thee.

Exodus 15:26

When we are on the road, we will encounter the regular dangers of being around other vehicles. We can watch and observe; we can admire the sunshine and the scenery; we can see the changes in the weather as we go from state to state, but we must always remember that we are not the ones driving!

It is the reign/rain of the enemy that makes the road dangerous. It is Satan's torrential reign/rain that makes it hard for us to see from our vantage point as the passenger. We have to trust that God knows the roads and that He knows how to drive. He knows how to avoid other vehicles that have gotten lost, are stuck, or that are broken down and still others that are making u-turns to go back in the other direction.

When we have sunshine, the road seems fine; things seem clear, but we should remember that we are still on the road. Just because there is sunshine does not mean that we can forget the fact that we are in the car. The fact that there is sunshine does not mean that the road is any less perilous; it only means that our view is not being obstructed. With sunshine, we can see the potential turns that are ahead and the curves that are in the highway. When the sun is shining, the signs are easy to see and the road ahead is open and *can* be inviting.

When Satan is reigning/raining, we are more apt to be cautious and are more tempted to ponder the *'what if's'* of the road. We want the driver to be careful; to slow down or to speed up; watch that sign or this one; turn here or there; or pull over so that we can rest. The reign/rain tends to pull us out of our comfort zone in the vehicle and that can be dangerous. We tend to want to side-seat drive and reach for the steering wheel.

> **"Take therefore <u>no thought for</u> the morrow: for the morrow shall take thought for the things of itself. Sufficient unto the day [is] the <u>evil</u> thereof."**

> Matthew 6:34

Sufficient means plenty, adequate, and enough for each day is the trouble that will happen in that day. We have to prevent ourselves from getting caught up in wanting to drive and control the vehicle. Remember, we are the children that are being taken to a destination that our Father has already mapped out; a destination that *He* knows and that *He* has been too previously. We must sit in our seats and continue to enjoy the ride there, no matter how long it may be.

When we get to where our Father is taking us, we can get out of the vehicle, stretch and say, *"Wow!" So this is it huh Dad?" "You said that this would be great, but Wow!" "Can I go exploring?"*

We will have gotten the experience of having traveled the road with our Father. We will have had the pleasure of having spent time with Him and enjoyed His company and protection. The road turned out to be only a means of transportation to get us to where He was taking us. Sure there was sunshine and that was good while it lasted. Sure there was rain/reign and that caused us to be apprehensive, but He got us through *all* of *that* unscathed.

Once we have gotten to our Father's destination, what we will recognize is the fact that, *"We can see clearly now; the rain/reign is gone!"*

Notes And Reflections For The Reader:

Notes And Reflections For The Reader:

Blessings Delayed

[God's answer is either:
Yes, No, or Wait]

"But the prince of the kingdom of Persia withstood me one and twenty days: but, lo, Michael, one of the chief princes, came to help me; and I remained there with the kings of Persia."

Daniel 10:13

[Before I get started on this chapter, I must digress and point out that one of the most popular video game series is called The 'Prince of Persia' and Hollywood has also made a movie with the same title. The enemy has been bold enough to make another video game where he states that this is a war! It is called the 'World of Warcraft'. I have heard and experienced what this game does to those that play. It is much like 'Dungeons and Dragons' where the players can lose themselves in role playing this game. A craft is what is commonly spoken of in Wicca to refer to the *practices* of witches and warlocks. This is why they call their belief and profession *'witchcraft'*.

I had to get that off of my chest since we are entering into the book of Daniel for this portion. The angel tells Daniel that his prayer was *answered* the moment that he prayed it, but there was spiritual warfare involved concerning the response. His prayer was delayed twenty-one days by the Prince of Persia.

God will say YES to our prayers as long as they are according to His will and His promises. He will say NO when they are *not* in line with His will. If the answer that we want will not benefit us; or if it will infringe on another person's *free will* then we can bet that it will be a resounding no. Our prayers are always answered, but it may also be that the enemy is playing a role in us receiving the response. It could be that it is simply not time for us to receive the answer. Either way God's answers fall into Yes, No, or Wait! Prayers can be answered very quickly if God wants the glory very quickly and the earthly response immediate like in the book of Exodus with Moses and Pharaoh or in Elijah's case with the prophets of Baal. When God wants to set a standard or prove Himself omnipotent, the answers to our prayers can be immediate and redemptive. There is nothing that is restraining God except for the fact that He is staying true to His Own Word. This is why Satan is able to operate in the way that we see and impact us so thoroughly at times. It is like a lawyer that will bend the rules of the law by seeking out loopholes. It may appear that the lawyer has a point; he may delay the outcome of the case; he may even buy his client time, but the law, however, does not change! God is the ultimate judge and He will see *justice* done.

We will **ask** God for all types of things, but are we reading His Word or praying that His will be done? Jesus prayed that His Father's will be done in earth as it is in heaven. If God's will is being done in heaven, on a continuous basis, then why not here in earth? It is because when Satan tricked Adam out of his dominion in Eden, the temporal rules changed; God's desired will concerning His creation changed.

In Eden, Adam had dominion over everything that God had created on earth; according to God's will. Adam was the benefactor of God's will with all of the inheritance that was to be given him. Satan stole that dominion and became the beneficiary; so the relationship that man had with the creator of the rules was severed. This was a loophole. Without the ability to maintain authority over what we were created to rule; man needed a mediator to negotiate the terms of the will. God established a New Will and Testament through His Son the mediator and advocate.

When someone has the power and authority to make a decision, then that decision is <u>final</u> unless it is superseded by the authority that **this** person is under. If the person that has been given authority gives their authority to someone else, then that other person may or may not submit to the greater authority. This is called the power of attorney and it can only be given away by the party that has that power. The rules have been set and the execution of those rules may not bind the new party in the ***same*** way as the former. An example would be that, an ambassador from another country is not always subject to all of the same rules as the *citizens* residing in the country to which they have been assigned. Should they make an error within the country to which they have been assigned, they are still citizens of the country from which they have been sent not the one in which they are currently on assignment. Someone else must then be called in to 'mediate' between the two countries, in order to bring about an agreeable resolution.

Maybe God has said YES to what His ambassador was trying to accomplish, but the error was God's ambassadors. The terms of what needs to be negotiated, will rest partially on each country. The *legal* aspect of the negotiation must be worked out with each side, since there is now a prisoner, but the ambassador's country will insist on having him/her being returned home safely.

The instruction on how to delegate their authority and how to proceed with their duties has already been outlined for the ambassador during his/her training. Any issue that falls outside of, what the ambassador has been trained to accomplish should be immediately communicated back to the ambassador's home country. This is where Adam made his mistake. Satan did not attack him directly, but rather indirectly. It's like coming back to your office and finding out that one of the players on your team has made an ***executive*** decision. Now the company is in trouble and the chief shareholder is angry; the CEO!

Had Adam proceeded in this way, then God could have told him YES, NO, or WAIT. Adam already knew his mandate, but he was caught in the crossfire. Should he follow the direction of a chief shareholder first or take the chance of letting his co-worker and friend pay the penalty imposed by both the chief shareholder and also by the foreign country?

There is no defined amount of time in scripture for which Adam walked with God before Eve was created; or between that time and their mutual sin. What we do know is that Satan also injected fear into this situation and Adam doubted God. The lack of trust in any relationship is always a precursor to negativity in the relationship and can prove its undoing.

"So God created man in his [own] image, in the image of God created he him; male and female created he them. And God blessed them, and God said unto them, Be fruitful, and multiply, and replenish the earth, <u>and subdue it</u>: and <u>have dominion over</u> the fish of the sea, and over the fowl of the air, <u>and over every living thing that moveth upon the earth</u>. And God said, Behold, I have given you every <u>herb bearing seed</u>, which [is] upon the face of all the earth, and every tree, in the which [is] the fruit of a <u>tree yielding seed</u>; to you it shall be for meat. And to every beast of the earth, and to every fowl of the air, and to every thing that creepeth upon the earth, wherein [there is] life, [<u>I have given</u>] every green herb for meat: and it was so."

Genesis 1:27-**30**

"And the LORD God took the man, and put him into the Garden of Eden to dress it and to keep it."

Genesis 2:15

"And out of the ground the LORD God formed every beast of the field and every fowl of the air; and brought [them] unto Adam to see what he would call them: and <u>whatsoever Adam called every living creature, that [was] the name thereof</u>. And Adam gave names to all cattle, and to the fowl of the air and to every beast of the field; but for Adam there was not found an help meet for him."

Genesis 2:19-**20**

> *And the rib, which the LORD God had taken from man, made he a woman, and brought her unto the man. And Adam said, This is now bone of my bones, and flesh of my flesh: she shall be called Woman, because she was taken out of Man.*

Genesis 2:22,23

[Forgive me Dear reader because for I am learning myself as I write these pages. The word of God is so rich and so deep that we should always remain teachable. It has just occurred to me that Eve was given the same command as Adam in Genesis 1:27-30 God gave them both the directive of how to live on the earth, but God did not give them the command concerning what trees not to eat of in Eden. That directive was mans. Adam was to instruct his wife and name her as well as God had given him that responsibility. Adam called her name _**wo-man**_ because she was taken out of man. Until then God called them both Adam. He later changed her name to *Eve* after the sin and because she would be the mother of all mankind living on the earth. It has also occurred to me that the tree of the knowledge of good and evil must have born a fruit that did not have seeds in order to reproduce itself. Every herb bearing seed and every tree bearing seed and every green herb was to be for meat/food for them. God says this twice in the same verse.

> *This is the book of the generations of Adam. In the day that God created man, in the likeness of God made he him;* <u>*Male and female*</u> *created he them; and blessed them, and* <u>*called their name Adam, in the day when they were created.*</u>

Genesis 5:1

Regardless of the amount of time that Adam spent with God, his mandate was clearly outlined in the beginning. The right to go back to God and ask for guidance was always there. He tried to make an *'executive'* decision without going through the proper channels. The worst response that God may have given him would have been 'Wait'. That would have only caused him to be in opposition with

Eve; he already knew that the correct response was No! The difficulty for Adam came in the form of someone else having to suffer the consequences of the mandate that *__he__* was given to delegate.

When we get our answers from God, they are clear and the only dilemma we face is whether or not we will be obedient. Yes or No is generally easy; Wait proves to be a problem for us because it involves patience and time. This is the reason that we go through trials and tribulation in life.

> *"And not only [so], but we glory in tribulations also: that __tribulation worketh patience__;"*

> Romans 5:3

> *"Knowing [this], that __the trying of your faith__ worketh patience."*

> James 1:3

Paul tells us in his letter, to the church in Rome, that our troubles are working out patience in us. This is almost always a WAIT answer from God. We will say, "God when? God how? God why?", and so on, in situations where we are immersed in trials. However, James tells us that God is trying our faith in these situations. He wants to know if we can handle His response to our prayers so that He will know where to position us on the battlefield. It is not that He doesn't already know our strengths and weaknesses; but a good 'Captain' will bring out the very best in His soldiers so that *they* will be confident in themselves as well.

Notes And Reflections For The Reader:

Notes And Reflections For The Reader:

Try the Spirits

Don't believe everything you hear

Beloved, believe not every spirit, but <u>try the spirits </u>whether they are of God: because many false prophets are gone out into the world.

1 John 4:1

Sometimes things look like one thing but, upon a closer look, they turn out to be something else. A simple rule to follow is that if something looks too good; sounds too good; acts to good or makes you feel too good, this is usually a reason to pause and think first! This is what trying the spirits will reveal. If we keep in mind that we should be watchful to test everything that does *not* line up with God's word, we can give ourselves a fighting chance.

How do we know what spirit is operating? We have to know God's *Word* and that will give us the discernment that we need. It will give us an inside track on what to look for; how to face it; and how to stand and persevere through it and against it.

One thing that works in the Spiritual, Mental, and Physical realms is that once something is learned, it becomes very difficult to unlearn. Once we have burned our fingers on a stove we have internalized the necessary precautions that will protect us in the future. When we learn how to execute a certain task, we must be re-trained in order to erase the training that we have internalized. In order to learn another form of execution, for a learned behavior, or mental behavior takes time and work. It is the same way with spiritual things.

Once we have the Word of God in our spirits, we are not only accountable for that knowledge, but it sets a standard against anything that is in opposition to it. If we turn against it, then we are forcing ourselves to be *re-trained* against God's will.

"Speaking lies in hypocrisy; *having their conscience seared with a hot iron;*"

1Timothy 4:2

My mother told me, a very long time ago, that when the truth is spoken it will resonate in our spirits. That is because *'truth'* is another characteristic of God that He has created in us like *love*.

During our walk, we will encounter so many different people. Each one has been created by God and has a purpose for their lives. Whether they have embraced that purpose or rejected it is one of the easiest things to determine. Should they have accepted or are seeking to please God, then we can see the character of God in their actions. They exemplify: integrity, morality, honesty, trustworthiness, perseverance, longsuffering, peace, and a host of other character traits that we are drawn too. Someone that has moved or is moving in a different direction will give us the impression, in our spirits, of someone that is pushing through a crowd in the wrong direction. It is like the salmon that swim 'upstream' to spawn. The river is moving, in the direction, in which the water has been designed to flow, but the salmon fight that natural flow to achieve their own purpose.

I will admit that this is becoming more and more difficult to identify in these last days. The spirit of anti-Christ has already gone out into the world. This spirit; this attitude; will fight any and everything that is written in the Word of God. It comes up against the smallest portion of scripture and the most obvious wrongs that God's word will point out. It will turn the *truth* into a *lie* and turn *wrong* into *right*. What we must do as soldiers is pull these ideas and imaginations down; force them to submit to the Word that we know. We must place them in a choke-hold and force them to submit to Christ. If we do not or feel as if we cannot, then who or what is commanding us?

>*"<u>Casting down imaginations</u> and <u>every high thing</u> that exalteth itself against the knowledge of God, and <u>bringing into captivity</u> every thought to the obedience of Christ;"*

>2 Corinthians 10:5

The type of spirit that we should be on the lookout for is one that attacks our *mind*; seeks to replace God, His Word, and His Spirit; and seeks to make itself the most important thing in our lives. We are to be good soldiers and take that spirit into captivity and bring it before Christ. The Word (Christ) will make that spirit yield and flee from you.

Remember how the demoniac reacted when Jesus was around?

>*"And, behold, <u>they</u> cried out, saying, "What have <u>we</u> to do with thee, Jesus, thou Son of God?" "Art thou come hither to torment <u>us</u> before the time?"*

>Matthew 8:29

The spirit of Anti-Christ will recognize the spirit of Christ! When people are giving you a hard time for no reason; when it seems that your trial is unreal or unnecessarily hard; when it seems like everyone is against you, then the spirit of Anti-Christ is in operation. When you feel like you have done everything right; you have prayed and shielded yourself from the worst, it is because you are in a battle.

>*And cried with a loud voice, and said, What have I to do with thee, Jesus, thou Son of the most high God? I adjure thee by God, that thou torment me not. For he said unto him, <u>Come out of the man, thou unclean spirit. And he asked him, What is thy name?</u> And he answered, saying, My name is Legion: for we are many.*

>**Mark 5:10**

*(One thing that has always amazed me about this scripture is that Jesus cast the spirit out and **then** He asked its name. I'm still trying to figure out how that appeared to the disciples?)*

Do not think that the attack cannot come from amongst supposed members of the body of Christ or from within the house of God. This is exactly where Satan and his followers love to be. Remember, they miss the presence of God; so around God's people and in God's house is exactly where they hang out.

It is the pastor's job to guard the flock that he is steward over; their job is to defend the sheep from the wolves. David got to the point in his shepherding where he was fighting lions, and tigers, and bears – Oh my! He was so on point with his shepherding duties that his boldness carried him from shepherd to soldier to king. It carried David to a place where he could be upset at the *spirit of fear* that the enemy had injected into the Israeli army. It caused him to challenge and defeat a giant Goliath and then go on to defeat many more giants. *[Did you ever wonder why David got five stones when he was going to fight Goliath? Goliath had brothers... David also killed: one of Goliath's brothers, Ish'bi–be'nob, Saph, and the giant with six fingers and six toes on each hand and on each foot. You can read more about David's conquests in 2 Samuel and in* 1 Chronicles. 20.4-8.]

Every spirit that confesses that Jesus has come in the flesh is of God. Be careful with these scriptures. The meaning is not what it appears:

Hereby know ye the Spirit of God: Every spirit that confesseth that Jesus Christ is come in the flesh is of God:

1 John 4:2

Gill's Exposition of the Entire Bible

For many deceivers are entered into the world... By whom are meant false teachers, who are described by their quality, "deceivers", deceitful workers, *pretending* to be ministers of Christ, to have a: value for truth, a love for souls, and a view to the glory of God, but lie in wait to deceive, and handle the word of God deceitfully; and by their quantity or number, "**many**", and so likely to do much mischief; and by the place where they were, they were "**entered into the world**"; or "gone out into the world", as the Alexandrian copy and some others, and the Vulgate Latin and Syriac versions read; See Gill on 1 John 4:1; and by their tenet, who confess not that Jesus Christ is come in the flesh; these were not the Jews who denied that Jesus was the Christ, though they would not allow that Christ was come in the flesh; but *these were some who bore the Christian name, and professed to believe in Jesus Christ, but would not own that he was really incarnate, or assumed a true human nature,* only in appearance; and denied that he took true and real flesh *of the virgin,* but only seemed to do so; and these are confuted by the apostle, 1 John 1:1; and upon everyone of these he justly fixes the following character. This is a deceiver and an antichrist; one of the deceivers that were come into the world, and one of the antichrists that were already in it; and who were the forerunners of *the man of sin,* and in whom the mystery of iniquity already began to work; for antichrist does not design anyone particular individual person, but a set of men, that are contrary to Christ, and opposers of him.

Gill recognizes that the spirit of Anti-Christ is both one person and a set of people in scripture. We will be able to pinpoint these people by knowing the word of God and His language. The word says that, *"...my sheep know my voice."*

> ***And when he putteth forth his own sheep, he goth before them, and the sheep follow him: for they know his voice.***

John 10:4

The real spirit of Anti-Christ is very subtle. There is a difference between the spirit of 'antichrist' and 'The Anti-Christ', the man of sin. The *spirit* or character is any spirit that opposes Jesus the Messiah. Satan will say that Jesus *was* a real person, but what will be denied is that He as God came in the flesh. These people will not deny that Jesus has actually come in the 'flesh', but rather what they have a problem with is the '*virgin birth*'. It is a very subtle difference to be certain, *or* is it? They will not have a problem with the fact that Jesus walked the earth; no problems that Jesus was a Jew; no problem with His teachings; no problem with the fact that He was a historical figure; and no problem with His crucifixion, but there is *always* a problem with His virgin birth through Mary. This is what scripture means when it says that everyone that does not *confess* that Jesus has come in the flesh; or rather that He was born of a virgin. This is the deceptive spirit of antichrist. It is also the primary deception of the movie 'The Davinci Code'.

That Jesus has *come in the flesh* and that He was *born of a virgin* will always be a cause to split hairs in secular thinking. Most will not deny that Jesus walked the earth, but ask them do they believe that He was born of a virgin; you might have a very drawn out discussion. Very subtle distinction to be sure, but we must remember that Satan is a liar and knows his craft very well. We must know our trade very well also. The Christian must be able to expound on scripture; give the reasons why Jesus' birth was necessary and how it came to pass.

This is why we have to try the spirits. The enemy will attempt to try and catch you on a technicality or even a single word if we're not careful; he did it to Eve by inserting the word __*not*__. Three letters placed together and inserted, into a sentence, in place of God's Word, changed history and nearly destroyed humanity.

> *And the LORD God commanded the man, saying, Of every tree of the garden thou mayst freely eat: But of the tree of the knowledge of good and evil, thou shalt not eat of it: for in the day that thou eatest thereof __thou shalt surely die__.*

> Genesis 2:16-**17**

> *And the serpent said unto the woman, Ye shall __not__ surely die:*

> Genesis 3:4

They, however did die the same day. Remember Methuselah? He lived to be almost a day in God's reality of days. A day with the lord

71

is as a thousand years and a thousand years is like a day. So man died exactly the same day as God told them in God's time table. ***And all the days of Methuselah were nine hundred sixty and nine years: and he died.***

Genesis 5:27

God said that if you eat from *this* tree, you **_will_** surely die. Satan said you will **_not_** surely die. This little word, led to a punishment on humanity, which has lasted for six thousand years. Satan was not tried and he was not tested concerning what he was bringing to the table with Adam. Satan did not line up with the Word of God and he should have been called on the carpet about that. He was not supposed to be addressing the man's wife apart from the man. Adam and all of humanity are paying the price.

Trying the spirits is a time when we are forced to think! It is a difficult application at first, but it grows with the growth of our relationship with God. The more of *His* Word we internalize, the more we become conformed to the image of His son Jesus. Then we grow to be one step closer toward being transformed by having our minds renewed. When our minds are renewed, it becomes more difficult for our enemies to tell us **_anything_** that they feel like telling us.

Over time, when we study to show ourselves approved by God, trying the spirits becomes a reflex. We will automatically question anything that sounds wrong and always have our spiritual ears open. The spirit of God will guard us; speak to our spirits; direct us in our responses and keep our feet on the straight and narrow.

> *"For kings, and [for] all that are in authority; that we may lead a quiet and peaceable life in all godliness and honesty. For this [is] good and acceptable in the sight of God our Savior; Who will have all men to be saved, and **to come unto the knowledge of the truth**. For [there is] one God, and one mediator between God and men, the man Christ Jesus;"*

1Timothy 2:2-**5**

It is God's desire that all men have salvation and come to the knowledge of the truth. This is so that they are first on their way to heaven and second able to try the spirits. A true and popular saying says: *"knowledge is power!"*

When people are obsessed, suppressed, or possessed by an evil spirit, the evidence is very clear. It was very easy to determine the state of the demoniac that lived in the tombs and cut himself with rocks. He was stronger than a normal man and broke free from chains and ropes that were meant to bind him. For someone that is oppressed, suppressed or obsessed with a demonic spirit, the task becomes more difficult.

Suppression: People that are suppressed by demonic spirits usually have a number of familiar spirits attached to them. These spirits are like unnecessary baggage that weigh the person down in certain areas of their life. They can get through some areas of their life very easily and other areas they run into walls every single time. Take certain people that have trouble with the opposite sex or same sex. These spirits are often accompanied by other familiar spirits consistently. Once a person looks at and becomes attracted to certain things that are not in God's sites, then the enemy will use the *darkness of this world* to blind you to the light of God's word. You are off track and in the jungle. To look at a woman and lust after a certain thing concerning her will allow the enemy to cause you to be attracted to any other woman that has the same similarities. If it is her hair, then all of a sudden the enemy will send multiple women with the exact same hairstyle, different lengths, different textures and different colors of all choices. He will also send women of different skin colors, heights, faces, shapes and so on with the same type of woman that you have been attracted too. So that your choices become increasingly difficult and confusing. He enemy is attempting to erase the way back to the original thing that may not have been enmity with God, but you are now finding a difficulty in getting out of the jungle. You are drawn away from your unit and cannot find your way back easily. People that have difficulty with certain habits or behaviors or even with truthfulness. All of these types of suppressing spirits stand in a soldiers way and prevent them from pressing forward on the battlefield. Think of it this way, when we are trying to press forward in what God is calling us too and we just can't seem to get over certain hurdles in life, then it is because those spirits are weighing us down and wrestling with us consistently. Paul tells us in

Ephesians 6:12 "For we <u>wrestle</u> not against flesh and blood, but against principalities, against powers, against *the rulers of the darkness of this world*, against spiritual wickedness in high *places.*" He then tells us whom we are *wrestling* against. I think that the most important clue concerning what the soldier must fight against in daily life are *the rulers of the darkness of this world.* This speaks about every wickedness that can twist, tie down and/or entrench the Christian soldier. We become oppressed when we fail to break free of these familiar spirits and then they entangle us in the darkness of this world.

Oppression: Everyone that has not accepted Jesus as Lord and believed on God's salvation through Jesus is oppressed. There are different levels of oppression, but the enemy will oppress us with every opportunity. He will use what he knows about us; our families; our friends; our co-workers; our neighbors; etc… He will use circumstances and people that we do not know; he will use what we do know and twist it and keep us bound with details. In scripture, these are called familiar spirits as well. These spirits attach themselves to us because they are *familiar* with everything about us. They are not like our friends who know the things about us that we *want* them to know. These spirits have the advantage of being ageless and in a different realm than us; they know details; details that would put the IRS database to shame.

Satan can oppress us with our eating habits; with our smoking habits; with our propensity to gamble; with the way we like to dress or style our hair or makeup; and any of our tendencies, predispositions, and/or inclinations. He will take our over confidence or our low self esteem and destroy us if he can. He will take the seemingly very small miniscule items and make them impassable mountains in our lives.

Oppression simply means that in some way, shape, or form our enemy has placed his foot on our necks and does not want to let us up.

Obsession: This is Satan's way of getting us to break one simple commandment; Thou shalt have no other Gods before me! When the things in this life draw us away from God, we can become obsessed with them. Satan will use these things to pull us into situations that he *already* controls and then he has us in a trap.

If he tempts us into the bar scene, then we can become obsessed with all of the other patrons who are looking to drink their problems away. We can become attracted to their similar problems; their similar life stories; and their worldview. Satan can use this to cause all kinds of problems for us in life with this simple landmine. We can become alcoholics; we can get into trouble with the law; we can become poor examples to our families and friends; we can begin to operate below standard on our jobs; and we can become promiscuous in our sexual encounters. We can become unstable in the simplest parts of our lifestyle. Eventually it will get to a point where we are incapable of being able to function without looking forward to the next encounter or opportunity for alcohol. Did you ever wonder why the places that sell strong drink have on their advertisement signs '*Wine and Spirits*'?

We can become obsessed with pornography and Satan will use this as well. We can start off looking at the things that we like to see and do and become attracted to other things. We are not realizing that we are seeing a lot more than we are actually taking note of. We can become attracted to different forms of sexual fantasies that will then become encounters. We can get to a position where we have left the road and are willing to try things we never thought that we would *ever* try.

We can become obsessed with thrill seeking to the point where it becomes a drug to us. Satan knows that our bodies release certain chemicals while we are having certain experiences in life. So he utilizes that against us. He will use that fact to drive us toward looking for the next thrill to gain the next high. He will make the next thrill very accessible and during that one thrill, kill us because we have forgotten about God.

Since God knows our enemies better than we do, He has outlined our best course of action in His Word through the people who had to suffer these attacks first. The disciples were not just set into place to spread the gospel; they were a template for us to follow. Jesus was their template, so they knew how dangerous these spirits are.

Trying the spirits and fighting what Satan was trying to prevent, cost each disciple his life. John was the only disciple that died of natural causes and we still do not know what spiritual battles he fought. Being incarcerated for life, on the prison island of Patmos, was probably bad enough!

Notes And Reflections For The Reader:

Notes And Reflections For The Reader:

Tumbleweeds

When You Don't Have Strong Roots

"And now also the ace is laid unto the root of the trees: therefore every tree which bringeth not forth good fruit is hewn down, and cast into the fire."

Matthew 3:10

"Even so every good tree bringeth forth good fruit; but a corrupt tree bringeth forth evil fruit."

Matthew 7:17

"A good tree cannot bring forth evil fruit, neither [can] a corrupt tree bring forth good fruit.

Matthew 7:18

"Every tree that bringeth not forth good fruit is hewn down, and cast into the fire."

Matthew 7:19

"Either make the tree good, and his fruit good; or else make the tree corrupt, and his fruit corrupt: for the tree is known by [his] fruit."

Mathew 12:33

"And when he saw a fig tree in the way, he came to it, and found nothing thereon, but leaves only, and said unto it, Let no fruit grow on thee henceforward for ever. And presently the fig tree withered away."

Matthew 21:19

"And now also the ace is laid unto the root of the trees: every tree therefore which bringeth not forth good fruit is hewn down, and cast into the fire."

Luke 3:9

"For a good tree bringeth not forth corrupt fruit; neither doth a corrupt tree bring forth good fruit."

Luke 6:43

"For every tree is known by his own fruit. For of thorns men do not gather figs, nor of a bramble bush gather they grapes."

Luke 6:44

"He spake also this parable; A certain [man] had a fig tree planted in his vineyard; and he came and sought fruit thereon, and found none. Then said he unto the dresser of his vineyard, Behold, these three years I come seeking fruit on this fig tree, and find none: cut it down; why cumbersome it the ground?"

Luke 13:6, 7

I know that these are a lot of scriptures, but necessary to make the point. God speaks to everyone in His own way and, at the same time, differently to each of us. Can I tell you that He scared me when He said one word; *"Tumbleweed!"*

That shook me to my core and made me want to ask more questions and study more in depth about what He was saying. I happened to be praying for someone at the time God said that to me and it was just *scary*.

Tumbleweed is actually a Russian thistle. It is a plant that has green, star-framed, thorny leaves that set the background for a violet star-burst flower. It also grows in the Arizona desert and other deserts across the United States.

As I was praying for this person and God spoke, I immediately knew what He was saying, but I did not want to accept it. Tumbleweed used to be a plant with roots and flowers. Now it is has dried up; the roots have been torn from the ground and it is being blown around the desert with the changing of the winds.

In the beginning, these plant's roots were firmly fixed in the earth and sought water, whenever there was water available. It stretched forth its branches toward the sun and even produced a beautiful flower. Now this plant is good for nothing whatsoever except to be torn into pieces small enough to build a fire.

Tumbleweeds are blown around the desert from place to place as the wind directs. There is no stability in tumbleweed; there is nothing to stabilize them; no roots from which it can thrive and derive nourishment. The leaves have long withered and the flowers that bloomed have died in the desert heat. There is no longer anything attractive about this Russian thistle; in fact, no one even pays attention to the fact that this tumbleweed was once a thriving, vivacious plant. Tumbleweed is now associated with being a product of the many things that have not or are on their way toward being a memory. Tumbleweed becomes a tragic part of everything else that eventually dies in the desert.

The sad part about God revealing this to me is that I could not come up with any way that tumbleweed could be saved. It cannot be replanted; it cannot be re-potted; it cannot grow new roots; it will never have leaves or beautiful flowers again. It is like the scripture says: "*...tossed to and fro with every wind of doctrine.*" This is definitely a terrible place to be!

The Word says that if the tree is not producing fruit, then it is good for nothing else accept to be cast into the fire and burned. That was a clear message that this person was clearly on the fast track to hell and there was nothing that I could do about it. This would take a clear miracle. What was I to say; what was I to do? The leaves were dried up and the blooms were dead. What used to be a root system had long ceased to be able to take water into the plant and feed the limbs. They would not be able to stretch forth and take hold of even the most fertile ground. If the tumbleweed was blown into the water by the wind, it could not drink. This thistle always wants to be around water, but it can only act like the plants around it. It can never be the plant that God intended it to be.

This was truly a bad place to be if we are relating this to Christianity. It means that the person was once a thriving flower and the circumstances of the desert have uprooted them. It means that they have ceased to reach deeper into the 'good' ground to obtain the water of the word. What used to be beautiful about them has now dried up and died. Their gifting could have been: ministry, evangelism, preaching, helps, mime, liturgical dance, or anything that was attractive about that person's walk with the Savior.

It could have been the desert sun that made them want to stop striving for good water. It may have been the lack of water that made them quit trying to grow deeper roots. It may have been the constant pressure of the dry desert wind that made them quit resisting the consistent tug and pull of everyday life. In any event they have given up and let go! They are now tumbleweeds and simply go with the flow and have no direction in life whatsoever. What a miserable end for a once beautiful plant. It exists in the deserts of our lives, but it is never recognized. It will get tangled with other tumbleweed and be attached for a while, but neither has the ability to provide anything sustaining for the other. As the winds of life continue to blow them across the desert, two tumbleweeds may separate or they may find themselves entangled for a season, but neither is of any purposeful use accept to be kindling for fire.

> *"And he spake many things unto them in parables, saying, Behold, a sower went forth to sow; And when he sowed, some [seeds] fell by the way side, and the fowls came and devoured them up: Some fell upon stony places, where they had not much earth: and forthwith they sprung up, because they had no deepness of earth: And when the sun was up, they*

were scorched; and because they had no root, they withered away. And some fell among thorns; and the thorns sprung up, and choked them: But other fell into good ground, and brought forth fruit, some an hundredfold, some sixtyfold, some thirtyfold. Who hath ears to hear, let him hear."

Matthew 13:3-**9**

This analogy should be recognized and prevented before the Russian thistle can get to the tumbleweed stage. Pastors should check the status of their flock to make sure that the heat of the desert is not drying them out. They should make sure that they are being watered with the word on a regular basis and that they are actually drinking it. They must make certain the roots are not only growing, but taking hold of good ground. They must be aware of the winds of change and that their flock is able to withstand the constant pressure, the bending and the twisting of these constantly changing winds. They must treat the thistles of their congregation in the same way that Adam was instructed to keep and tend Eden.

Tumbleweed is reminiscent of the scripture that tells us of the coming great apostasy; the falling away from the church.

"Let no man deceive you by any means: for [that day shall not come], except there come a <u>falling away</u> first, and that man of sin be revealed, the son of perdition;"

But she was plucked up in fury, she was cast down to the ground, and the <u>east wind dried up her fruit: her strong rods were broken and withered; the fire consumed them.</u>

Ezekiel 19:12

This was how I felt after having ended that prayer It was all going to have to remain in the masters hands. We all want to take up tumbleweeds and replant them, but only a skilled potter could do the miraculous. My advice is to take the tumbleweed ton Him and then see what He and will do with the Russian thistle.

Notes And Reflections For The Reader:

Notes And Reflections For The Reader:

Tree Mentality vs. Vine Mentality

Where Am I Getting My Nourishment?

God looks at a great many things in scripture from the standpoint of a farmer or someone who loves plants. Think about that for a moment. God created the entire universe, but when He created the one being that was to be just like He was; in *His* likeness and in *His* image; He chose to place him in a garden.

God created the sun, the moon, the galaxies, and this planet earth, and then He chooses to set Adam in the Garden of Eden, with his wife, to keep it and tend to it. God's plan was to walk with and talk with His friend Adam in *His* own garden. No matter how you slice it, this plan is very peaceful and it *was* perfect! Adam's job was simple; tend the garden; enjoy your wife; make babies and fellowship *with* and be a son *to* God.

Like a gardener, God loves what He plants. His intention is to: nurture, cultivate, take care of, prune, and to love them and watch them grow and thrive. God even compares and views men as trees.

> *"And he cometh to Bethsaida; and they bring a blind man unto him, and besought him to touch him. And he took the blind man by the hand, and led him out of the town; and when he had spit on his eyes, and put his hands upon him, he asked him if he saw ought. And he looked up, and said, <u>I see men as trees, walking</u>. After that he put [his] hands again upon his eyes, and made him look up: and he was restored, and saw every man clearly."*

Mark 8:22-**25**

Jesus' power healed the blind man to the effect that he could see into the spiritual realm. The blind man saw people in the way that God sees people; as '*trees*'. From that point, the blind man's **mentality** was changed.

God looks at mankind as trees that bear fruit; either good or bad. That *fruit* would be our '*works*'. If we bear good fruit then we become the type of trees that God wants in His garden. If we bear bad fruit *or* if we produce no fruit, then God states that we are good for nothing except to be cut down and thrown into the fire; that would be hellfire. This is a sad commentary for those who simply refuse to accept the truth.

> *"Either make the tree good, and <u>his</u> fruit good; or else make the tree corrupt, and his fruit corrupt: for the tree is known by [<u>his</u>] fruit."*

Matthew 12:33

> *"And now also the ace is laid unto the <u>root</u> of the trees: every tree therefore <u>which bringeth not forth good fruit</u> is hewn down, and cast into the fire."*

Luke 3:9

The scripture does not say that the ax is laid to the tree itself, the way that one would usually fell a tree, but rather that the ax is laid to the *root*. God is serious about getting every trace of this type of tree out of His garden.

The scripture also does not say *<u>its</u>* fruit; it says *<u>his</u>* fruit. This proves to us that God sees us as trees. The identifying persona is that of a human being. God says that we are to make ourselves good and have good works or make ourselves corrupt and our works corrupt. Why? There is no straddling of the fence with God; no being lukewarm.

> *"So then because thou art lukewarm, and neither cold (corrupt) nor hot (good), I will spue thee out of my mouth."*

Revelation 3:16

If you are not exemplifying the qualities of either a good tree or a bad tree, then God does not want you as a part of His garden; period!

This is the ***tree mentality***; to grow in the forest amongst the other trees and hope that the woodsman will not notice them or either overlook him/her. The tree mentality is to blend in; to skate through; to not be recognized for the type of tree that it truly is. The tree mentality gets its nourishment from whatever source will promise water, sunlight, and air. There is never any consideration given to where the source of the water is; no question about the light source; these trees never smell the air that they are breathing. These things prevent the tree from growing as tall and as strong as it can. In fact, its growth is stunted and the tree becomes twisted and misshapen over time.

Satan on the other hand is more like a 'landscaper' than a gardener. He is more interested in changing the natural use of the foliage to make it suit his plans and his architecture. Trees and plants will be manipulated to compliment the landscape that *he* desires. They in effect will become perverted. Trees are bent when they are young so that they will grow in a certain way or in a certain direction. Plants are trimmed into different shapes that will accent *his* buildings or *his* landscape. They have cages placed around them so that they can only grow to a certain size; they are attached to wires, so that they can be manipulated into spreading their branches in ways that they were not meant too. They are kept alive only until they have fulfilled Satan's purpose and then they are uprooted and replaced by a different sapling. Think about what I am writing here and then think about the way that young people are being handled nowadays.

The ***vine mentality*** is different. The vine mentality is to become a productive part of a tree that is already growing. So if a tree is dying, the portion that is still alive and healthy can be cut off and grafted onto an established healthy tree with strong roots. The part that has been grafted in can now receive the right kind of nourishment, sunlight, and water that has made the healthy tree as tall and as strong as it has grown.

> *"I am the <u>true vine</u>, and my Father is the husbandman (gardener)."*

John 15:1

The following is how Paul explains the vine mentality along with all of its benefits and profits.

> *"And if some of the branches be broken off, and thou, being a wild olive tree, were gaffed in among them, and <u>with them partakes of the root and fatness of the olive tree</u>; Boast not against the branches. But if thou boast, thou nearest not the root, but the root thee. Thou wilt say then, The branches were broken off, that I might be gaffed in. Well; <u>because of unbelief they were broken off</u>, and thou staidest by faith. Be not high minded, but fear: For if God spared not the natural branches, [take heed] lest he also spare not thee. Behold therefore the goodness and severity of God: on them which fell, severity; <u>but toward thee, goodness, if thou continue in [his] goodness</u>: <u>otherwise thou also shalt be cut off</u>. And they also, if they abide not still in unbelief, shall be gaffed in: for God is able to gaff them in again. For if thou wet cut out of the olive tree which is wild by nature, and wet <u>gaffed contrary to nature into a good olive tree</u>: how much more shall these, which be the natural [branches], be gaffed into their own olive tree?"*

Romans 11:17-**24**

Paul reminds us that we are 'wild' trees meaning not from the nation of Israel. God, however, has made a way for us to receive the same benefits. He tells us that we can be '*grafted*' in through Jesus and receive what the original tree will receive. He reminds us not to get big heads and speak against the original olive tree or we will not receive those benefits. He also reminds us of the benefits that we are now getting by being grafted in and that the other branches have been broken off because of unbelief. If God broke off the **original** branches, be careful, because we are not recognizing how good the gardener is and how severe he can be when he needs to prune. God will cut off the ones that were grafted in also if they do not prove to be productive or He can graft back in the ones that were initially cut off.

> *And I heard the number of them which were sealed: and there were sealed an hundred and forty and four thousand of all the tribes of the children of Israel*

Revelation 7:4

These are the nation of Israel being grafted
back into the original Olive tree.

The vine mentality is appreciative of the fact that they did not have to die and dry up without water; whether without sunlight or suffocate without air. They recognize the tree that they were grafted into and that they can begin a new life as part of a healthy tree. They can grow to a place where they can be productive and bear fruit like they were intended too. Where the *tree mentality* is to survive by any means necessary; the *vine mentality* is *grateful* that the way to survive has been made available without the struggle.

So where are you getting your nourishment? Is it from Jesus, the '*true vine*' or from trying to blend into the forest with the other trees and by constantly fighting for what you believe will keep you alive? My goal is to not become **firewood** at the end of the day!

Notes And Reflections For The Reader:

Notes And Reflections For The Reader:

Notes And Reflections For The Reader:

The Valley Experience

The *Shadow* of Death – There are Giants Here

"And the border went up by the <u>valley</u> of the son of Hinton unto the south side of the Website; the same [is] Jerusalem: and the border went up to the top of the mountain that [lithe] before the <u>valley</u> of Hinton westward, which [is] at the end of the <u>valley</u> of the giants northward..."

Joshua 15:8

Sometimes we start off on a peak and must travel down the mountain to go through a valley. This is where we will begin to climb again in order to get to the next peak.

It took a certain amount of faith, to get from where we started on the ground, to get to the mountain top that we presently enjoy. God however does not want us to enter a *comfort zone* there. Christians are 'mountain climbers' and so when we have mastered one mountain, God expects us to prove to the entire world that the next mountain can be climbed.

What proves to be difficult for us, in our thinking is that, we tend to forget that climbing mountains is *what we do*. We have *learned* to climb, learned to set up peak camp; we know how to get comfortable; we have our supplies and our radio works fine; that part is easy! We just do not want to set up base camp again during the downward journey from our present peak. We get lazy and do not want to begin again! For some reason we have forgotten that this is <u>what we do</u>.

The valley experience can be trying. The sun doesn't reach all parts of the valley whereas the mountain top is covered with sunshine. The

94

mountaintop is warm and there is a certain amount of security away from predators and falling rocks. The valley gets dark and cold; it can be scary and perilous. The shadow of *death* is on every side, even when the sun is at its highest point in the heavens. Even though it is, our sustenance is found in the valley where the water flows. We must come down to get green food and we must come down to get water.

That is all that the 'shadow of death' is; a *shadow*. A shadow can make us cold, but we have packed our coats and warm clothing accordingly. The shadow can cause us to search for the sun, but we have packed our flashlights if necessary and know how to build a fire. Predators will threaten us in the darkness; they can even growl, but we have brought items with us that can be used for defense.

We should approach our mountain and valley experiences the same way as David. He was a shepherd and he knew how to lead, take care of, and defend his flock.

> *"Yea, __though I walk through the valley of the shadow of death__, I will fear no evil: for thou [art] with me; thy rod and thy staff they comfort me."*

Psalm 23:4

For we wrestle not against flesh and blood, but against principalities, against powers, against the rulers of the darkness of this world, against spiritual wickedness in high places. Wherefore take unto you the whole Armour of God, that ye may be able to withstand in the evil day, and having done all, to stand. Stand therefore, having your loins girt about with truth, and having on the breastplate of righteousness; And your feet shod with the preparation of the gospel of peace; Above all, taking the shield of faith, wherewith ye shall be able to quench all the fiery darts of the wicked. And take the helmet of salvation, and the sword of the Spirit, which is the word of God: praying always with all prayer and supplication in the Spirit, and watching thereunto with all perseverance and supplication for all saints.

God has given us the necessary weapons to fight any enemy in the valley. We are not to fear evil during our valley experiences; we are to recognize that God is always with us. When we must go down and through the valley, we must take a step back and see it for what it truly is. We are mountain climbers and we have been trained for this!

Whatever we have **not** learned should not dissuade us from moving forward in our chosen profession. We always have a guide to show us or remind us of what we should be doing; how to do it; and in which direction to go. The way that I like to look at it is; this is why it is called a *profession* of our faith.

> *Let us hold fast the *profession* of [our] faith without wavering; (for he [is] faithful that promised...)*

Hebrews10:23

We know that we have been trained and we know that we have climbed mountains before; what we have to remember now is that we will be going back down the mountain that we have already climbed for the purpose scaling the next one. We also must remember that, in order to get to the next mountain we must go through the valley.

We will question the fact that we have to pack up our tent; pack up our gear and food; and begin the descent down the mountain toward the valley. Yes, it is a lot of work, but the work will be worth the ascent of the next mountain that we have to climb. The mountain that we are on was scaled fairly easily because we have had pioneers that have paved the way before us. We have followed in the footsteps of the people that have previously scaled the same mountain. What becomes difficult is when we think too much about the work of climbing the next mountain that lies ahead of us. We tend to think of the work of getting the ropes our of or bag; about getting the boots that we will need to wear; about getting the connections and hooks that we will need; and trying to factor in everything that we believe will be required for the new mountain. Some items must be left behind; they will weigh us down. Some items must be swapped out for new ones. Some gear will have to be exchanged for the latest in mountain climbing equipment. All of these things have to be taken into consideration prior to beginning our climb down.

Once we have begun our descent, and reached the bottom; we must face the valley! We never start off in the valley before we start climbing, we start off at the base of the mountain on the pleasant side where we can still turn around and see the road and the city that we have left behind. The vehicle that brought us to the base of the mountain is still in sight and everyone is wishing us well.

On the valley side, we have nothing familiar that we can identify with. There is nothing on the valley side that looks recognizable and we are cautious with every step that we take forward. We know where we are going and our GPS is taking us in the right direction, but what lies around every turn is a mystery.

The thing that we have to move past in our minds is the 'shadow of death'. We have to know beyond any doubt that our team at 'home-base' is aware of our situation and they are watching our journey and checking our direction. We have to trust our team because they want to see us succeed and get to the top of the next precipice.

> *"And now, behold, <u>the LORD hath kept me alive</u>, as he said, these forty and five years, even since the LORD spake this word unto Moses, while [the children of] Israel wandered in the wilderness: and now, lo, I [am] this day fourscore and five years old. <u>As yet I [am as] strong this day as [I was] in the day that Moses sent me: as my strength [was] then, even so [is] my strength now, for war, both to go out, and to come in</u>. Now therefore <u>give me this mountain</u>, whereof the LORD spake in that day; for thou headrest in that day how the Anaheim [were] there, and [that] the cities [were] great [and] fenced: <u>if so be the LORD [will be] with me, then I shall be able to drive them out, as the LORD said</u>."*

> Joshua 14:10-**12**

Adopt Caleb's attitude toward the valley and the next mountain. Caleb was strong enough at eighty-five years old to go out fight wars and come back. He fought with his country in the battles that they had to fight upon entering the Promised Land. At eighty-five years old he had the right mindset to climb the next mountain and war with the giants. Caleb was willing to battle the giants in their own valley and he was prepared to climb the next mountain and take it from the giants that lived there as well.

Giants represent the things in our life that appear to be too large for us to prevail against. Giants represent our fears, our obstacles, our hindrances and everything that is trying to prevent us from reaching the peak of the mountain.

Caleb trusted God's Word that the next mountain would be his for an inheritance. Caleb wanted what was due him and he wasn't going to allow anything to stand in his way. If he had to brave the valley, then that was something he was willing to do. Climbing the mountain was something that he looked forward to doing because the prize that God promised was what awaited him.

The things that come up against us in the valley experience are no different than the giants that we face everyday; they are just in different places. The landscape is what makes us leery. The unfamiliar sounds and the darkness are what we are apprehensive about, but we must step back and remind ourselves that shadows are being manifest by *familiar* things only in the absence of light. The valley is where there seems to be a slowing down of the directions that we are used to getting to very quickly from our team. We may make a call and have to wait on an answer. This is because we are in the valley and the signal is faint, but it *is* still there. The walls of the valley hinder our signal from getting to us immediately, but it has been sent. We feel as if we are moving slowly because we are being overly cautious, but we are making forward progress. This is called *lateral* movement. It is neither up nor down, but it is rather <u>*through*</u>. David said, ***"Yea though I walk <u>through</u> the valley of the shadow of death…"*** He knew that he had to walk through, but it was only on the way to his destination.

If it is the valley of the giants, then we will have to fight our way through. We still must rely on our team and the signal that we *are* receiving. The team will never leave us or forsake us; the team is well aware of the valley experience. A giant may appear in the form of our spouse; one may appear in the form of our children; one may appear in the form of our job, but if we have packed the right equipment we can get *through* the valley.

Our team has a different vantage point than we do, but they cannot carry us through the valley. Walking through the valley is something that we must do on our own. We have to check our compass and GPS more often in the valley. We have to look for things in the valley that can threaten or prevent us from getting to the next mountain. However, there will come a time when we will be able to see the base of the next mountain. There will come a time when we have to unpack our rope; our mountain climbing gear; and our warm clothing and food for the climb. This is where we can begin our ascent. This is where we can leave the valley experience behind us and focus our efforts on looking up!

We must remember that it took faith to get us to the top of the first mountain; now we will have to climb the next mountain in faith as well!

> *"For therein is the righteousness of God revealed from <u>faith</u> to <u>faith</u>: as it is written, The just shall live by faith."*

Romans 1:17

Notes And Reflections For The Reader:

Notes And Reflections For The Reader:

The P's of the Christian Walk

The Cake has to have <u>All</u> of the Ingredients?

We cannot skip any steps in the <u>process</u> if we are to honor God.

Christians have problems; or didn't you think so? Well if you didn't already know; we do! The difference between our problems and the world's problems is that we have ***hope***. The world may offer all sorts of things, but worldly, hope that *can* be trusted, is a myth; a farce; it is hype. The offer is ever there, yet it is only attainable for a price that no one is truly willing to pay!

The hope of the world is not worth your happiness; your peace of mind; your honesty or your integrity. It is not worth your health or your sanity. It is not worth your self-esteem; and it is not worth your reputation or your name. These are the things that must often be given up while chasing the lie of worldly hope. Hope in wealth, hope in happiness, hope in prosperity, hope in comfort and security, and hope in eternity are some of the things that the world will deceive us into believing that it can provide. This is very, very far from reality, if you think about it.

People in the world do so many things to gain wealth. Yet they often lose everything that is truly valuable to achieve that very goal. The more that wealth is chased, the more that must be given up to attain and hold on to it. Even people that win the lottery are not able to retain their windfall for very long. Holding on to and being able to manage money is something that requires experience and training. Those that have been born into wealth are taught these lessons at a very early age in life. They know how to secure their wealth and make it work for them.

A prime example is Donald Trump. He is the son of New York City Real real-estate developer Fred Trump. He *has* had to file for bankruptcy and yet, he never missed a step. This is all because he knows *how* to make money. He has been trained in how to create and manage his finances.

Dame Elizabeth Rosemary "Liz" Taylor was a Hollywood actress that died with a net worth of more than $1 billion dollars. Her hope wasn't only in money, but in wanting the world's brand of security. She was married eight times to seven different men and never seemed to grasp what she seemed to be looking for in life – **security**!

Michael Jordan, Kobe Bryant, Michael Vic, Tiger Woods, Ray Lewis, O.J. Simpson and a whole host of other professional athletes have made a worldwide name for themselves in sports. They are like the ancient Greeks that focused on building their bodies and honing their athletic skills to participate in the decathlon games. Each one of these star athletes has had tragedy and embarrassment strike their lives and all of there fame and money still cannot give them comfort; they cannot achieve true happiness.

These people and many more are chasing the world's hope and getting exactly what the world is willing to pay; sorrow! They are finding themselves in a different spotlight and have become fodder for the media and paparazzi. They become the next foolish person who had it all and lost it; got someone killed or witnessed someone being killed; or simply ended up with a lifetime of regrets.

We can only hope that people will follow us in our faith because; if the Christian does not have anything else; we have a true hope; real hope!

"That at that time ye were without Christ, being aliens from the commonwealth of Israel, and strangers from the

> *covenants of promise, <u>having no hope, and without God in</u> <u>the world</u>..."*

Ephesians 2:12

Paul tells these worldly minded persons that they are without salvation from their sinful nature and are not the beneficiaries of God's promises. He tells them that they have no hope and are without their Creator in this world.

Paul pretty much summed it up in one phrase; the hope that they think that the world can provide, is no hope at all because God has been excluded.

There are five P's that will definitely help those who are willing to pay attention:

THE 5 P's
1. For every <u>problem</u>,
2. There is a Godly <u>principle</u>,
3. Which leads to a Godly <u>provision</u>,
4. Which leads to a godly/spiritual <u>promise</u>
5. We cannot skip any steps in the <u>process</u> if we are to honor God

I have stated previously that Christians have *problems* like everyone else. We understand that for each problem that we have, there <u>is</u> a Godly *principle* that will address it. God in His divine omnipotence has also provided a *provision* and a *promise* that we can count on. We tend to want to skip from problem to promise instead of going through the whole *process* so that we are able to learn during the course of the journey.

Sampson was under the Nazareth vow. The problem was that Israel needed a judge and a champion to fight off their enemies the Philistines. The Nazareth vow was a priestly vow, which Sampson's parents raised him in, and Sampson was blessed through this. He was not to cut his hair; he was not to drink strong drink; and he was not to touch any dead thing. These were the principles and the conditions that God set into place. The provision was that Sampson would have unnatural strength and the promise was that he would easily defeat Israel's enemies; which he did.

Sampson moved out of his priestly calling to obtain a woman that he should not have. He did not know that her intention was to discover his weakness. While he slept, she cut his hair and caused him to side-step a part of the process; a part of his Godly vow.

Sampson was in God's graces until Delilah caused him to move past the *process* that placed him in position to judge and defend Israel. Only through prayer was Sampson able to regain his strength, but his price was his eyes. As I have previously stated; this is one of Satan's tricks the lust of the eye. This was the very thing that got him off of track in the first place. However, God is faithful and even though Sampson's lesson was harsh, he did better in his death than in his life!

Sure we all have problems, yet we must find out God's principle for that problem. If we do **this** then God will do **that**. What are God's provisions for being obedient? This is our next step. After we find out what His provisions are, then we must inquire about the promises that are associated with the things that He wants to bless us with. We need to understand that we have a role to play in our own blessings and God does have His requirements. He is not a Genie in a bottle. One thing that will surely shipwreck us is trying to take shortcuts. The entire process must come to fruition or we tie God's hands because He will not act against His own word.

Let's look at one more person; the apostle Paul. Why was Paul a problem? Paul was killing Christians! Paul considered himself to be a Pharisee of the Pharisees; in other words, the best of the best. He was leading the way against anyone that taught anything other than what the Mosaic Law had stipulated. When Jesus came on the scene, He brought a different spin to the Pharisees teaching. This 'new' doctrine was unacceptable to the Pharisees and against Paul's training. These 'new' followers of Jesus were to be summarily hunted down and put to death.

For Paul, the threat, that he felt that Jesus posed to his religion, was the problem. Jesus corrected Paul and pointed out that his approach to the perceived problem was in fact the problem. Paul overlooked the key principle that God's promise was to send a Savior and the Jews were the ones that were missing it. The Israelites had their eyes on the wrong prize; a selfish prize.

Because of their captivity under Roman rule, they looked for God to free them from their captors again. They looked for the promise of God sending an earthly King for their country and not a savior for mankind. They were looking for Yeshiva Ben-David (The Messiah the son of David the King) and not Yeshiva Ben-Cayuse (Jesus, the Messiah, the son of Joseph the carpenter). Jesus' earthly kingdom was not to begin until the completion of God's process. God's plan was to redeem mankind and fulfill His promise to His friend Abraham.

> *"And in thy seed <u>shall all the nations of the earth be blessed</u>; because thou hast obeyed my voice."*

Genesis 22:18

> *"And the scripture, foreseeing that God would justify the heathen through faith, preached before the gospel unto Abraham, [saying], <u>In thee shall all nations be blessed</u>."*

Galatians 3:8

The Israelites were tired of being oppressed and wanted their promised king, but they forgot about the promise that God made to their father Abraham. God will not expect us to hold fast to the *process* and not adhere to it Himself. They could not receive their blessing until God's full promised process was fulfilled.

The Godly provision was that people, who were not a part of God's chosen nation, were given access to the benefits of the same promise. Paul, even being a Pharisee, missed what was laid out in the very first chapter of God's Word. The curse that was placed on Adam and Eve affected everyone that would ever be born on this planet and God's promise of a savior needed to be fulfilled first.

Paul became one of the greatest apostles of the Bible by accepting the fact that he had skipped a vital step in the process. He missed the Jesus part of the process.

Identify the problem; identify God's principle for correcting the problem; what are the provisions for the problem and then we can count on the promises of God coming to pass. Do not forget that there is a process!

If we want to bake a cake, we have to use all of the ingredients!

Notes And Reflections For The Reader:

Notes And Reflections For The Reader:

The Fear Bomb

Feel Free to Cover Your Ears

"Mn's <u>hearts failing them for fear</u>, and for looking after those things which are coming on the earth: for the powers of heaven <u>shall</u> be shaken."

Luke 21:26

I immediately think of two things when I read this scripture. The first is that, in the end times, men will have heart attacks when they begin to see the signs and wonders in the heavens. The next is that people's compassion (heart) for the gospel and for the things that are righteous will not allow them to have the courage required to stand up against injustice and evil. I believe that both ideas are right; one literally and one figuratively.

Fear is one of Satan's favorite weapons. He uses this to intimidate and convince his adversaries to abandon hope. He uses fear to persuade them to give up before the battle has begun. This is a weapon of Satan's that is very effective on those who do not have a relationship with God. When we know that our Father is the biggest and strongest man in the neighborhood, we don't have the same apprehensions that the other neighborhood children may have; we are confident and feel safe.

Fear is a restraint; it is like any binding tool that has been designed to hold you in place while someone else controls you. Fear can prevent you from doing almost everything. It can keep you from speaking when you ought to say what is on your mind. It can prevent you from moving in the right direction or in any direction or simply quench your motivation to move. Fear can make you act out of character and place you into situations that would otherwise be avoidable. It can stop you from making clear and concise decisions.

One of the most obvious examples of fear today is the inability to be able to listen to the gospel; the good news that there *is* another way. This is the fear of being accountable to God and His wrath, but there is a difference between paralyzing fear and reverential fear. People are simply afraid of everything and they are struggling to keep straight faces. They are afraid of losing their jobs, their homes, their marriages and families, their way of life, their manner and quality of living. Afraid of losing their health, their culture, their race, basically their comfort zones.

I have never seen so many people refuse to listen to what is clearly right; clearly the truth. People are now listening to any and everything that will make them feel good and ease their fears about life. People are so scared that they are looking for a way to escape the real world. If they can redirect their focus to something that will allow them to not face reality, then they will grab hold of that and live in an alternate reality; in a fantasy.

The Word of God carries with it an accountability and truth that must be considered in a wicked world. Remember, man was created in the image and likeness of God. This alone should make us afraid of any consequences that may be associated with sin, in a world where Satan is trying to erase that connection. These are the times when the lines are being drawn in the sand and God is insisting that sides must be taken. If Satan succeeds in erasing the natural lines that God has placed in His plan, then it can become very hard for people to know which side that they are on. In my opinion, it is better to be as far on the right side as humanly possible. It will be sad to find out that we were too close to the wrong side when the distinguishing line is erased. We could find ourselves in the enemy's camp and then it will be too late.

God has not given us the spirit of fear; that spirit comes from God's enemy. What our Father has given us is His Spirit.

> *"For God hath not given us the spirit of fear; but of power, and of love, and of a sound mind."*

2 Timothy 1:7

I have often wondered why He gave us these three in this particular order. We need the ***power*** of God's Holy Spirit residing in us because of what Satan can accomplish through fear. With power comes the ability to resist fear and the paralyzing effect that it can have on us. Fear can render us power<u>less</u> to the tricks of the enemy, so God gives us the power to stand against this first. God is trying to make us power<u>ful</u>. John tells us that fear has torment and suffering. *This* is what the enemy wants to do to us through fear.

> ***"There is <u>no fear in love</u>; but <u>perfect love caster out fear</u>: because fear hath torment. He that fearful is not made perfect in love."***

1 John 4:18

With the number of things to consider in today's world; the many different avenues that lead us in the direction of fear; is it any wonder why man doesn't want to deal with life? Everything in today's world has become something to be afraid of and with that fear comes suffering. We will most definitely need power to stand through and endure the many different things that are thrown at us in a world that is changing this fast. We will need power to fend off the mental attacks and mind games that the enemy will hurl at us to weaken our will. I have to feel sad for those people that will not accept the Word of God so that they can have His power. I feel bad because they have to suffer because they are living in fear.

They will follow Satan down a very dark winding road to hell in order to escape the suffering caused by fear. They will try to party it away; turn the music up louder and dance until their legs hurt. They will try to drink it away; thinking if I drink enough I won't have to think about my problems and I will have people to talk too. They will try to immerse themselves in work and only deal with the day to day bills; thinking "I can forget about what's going on in the world." They will try to go to church and hope that God will give them a good mark for trying; but without faith it is impossible to please God! They only end up being fearful church goers that feel secure on Sunday and Wednesday. God is probably wondering, *"Why did you come to my house?"*

"But without faith [it is] impossible to please [Him]: for he that cometh to God must believe that He is, and [that] He is a retarder of them that diligently seek Him."

Hebrews 11:6

We will get the first component of power; next God has given us His *perfect **love*** as a second spiritual component. Having love within us also gives us the ability to establish our defenses against fear.

A mother's love will brave anything to protect her children; she will stand against things that would make a grown man run. A father's love will make him run into a burning building to save his family and forget about the danger of the flames. These are examples of the closest that man can come to perfect love.

*"He that loveseat not knoweth not God; for **God is love**."*

1 John 4:8

*"And we have known and believed the love that God hath to us. **God is love** ; and he that dwelleth in love dwelleth in God, and **God in him**."*

1 John 4:16

The reason that love is one of the things that God gives us is because His love is so strong that it repels fear. It actually casts it out! If Satan is attempting to use the fear bomb to destroy you, God's love will diffuse it.

Having the love of God will increase your power. It will give you abilities that you did not know that you had. It will allow you to endure the seemingly impossible. Having love will give you strength that will keep you upright when others would have fallen. Love will allow you to overlook wrongs committed against you and make you appreciate the things that are good in life.

> *"And above all things have fervent charity among yourselves: for charity <u>shall cover the multitude of sins</u>."*

1 Peter 4:8

Fervent means: enthusiastic, passionate, zealous. Love will allow you to look at a sinner through God's eyes and cause you to recognize their need for a savior. Love lets us pity people who have not taken hold of the free gift of God in Christ Jesus. We do not accept their sin, but we can look past what the enemy is doing in their lives and identify that God has created them for a purpose. It gives us a Godly compassion and desire that makes us desire to prevent Satan from claiming their lives.

Love gives us Godly vision. It makes us see things from a *positive* perspective instead of the *negative* perspective that fear tries to show us. It makes us people that have the ability to move through and past insurmountable odds. In love, we become *over-comers* instead of *under achievers*. It is the God in us that is the component that drives Satan away.

> *"Nay, in all these things we are more than conquerors through him that <u>loved us</u>."*

Romans 8:37

The third component is a **sound mind**. Without a sound mind, the enemy can impose his complete will upon us and tell us whatever he wants us to believe. For those who do not have a sound mind, they are basically Satan's pawns. He can move them around as he sees fit and get the other pieces to follow them. The old saying is, "Birds of a feather flock together." Notice how the enemy will keep weak minded people; people with the same issues; hurting people in the same company and prevent them from being able to free themselves.

This is because they are not sound minded. Their thinking is not stable and their focus tends to be split. Their concentration is usually on themselves or their perception of themselves and their problems. The Lord also calls them double-minded because they are volleying back and forth between two patterns of thought. In today's vernacular we might call this bipolar.

> *"If any of you lack wisdom, let him ask of God, that given to all [men] liberally, and upbraiding not; and it shall be given him. But let him ask in faith, nothing wavering. For he that waverer is like a wave of the sea driven with the wind and tossed. For let not that man think that he shall receive any thing of the Lord. A <u>double minded man [is] unstable in all his ways.</u>"*

> James 1:5-**8**

If we find ourselves to be wavering between two ways of thinking; being pulled in two different directions, then we must ask God for wisdom. Wisdom is one of the things in His word that he will continually give you and not hold back. James says that He will gladly give you wisdom liberally. Think about King Solomon, who had God's favor to ask for anything that he wanted and he chose wisdom, to be able to lead the people of God in the right fashion. With that request came anything else that he could have ever asked of God. In asking God for wisdom, Solomon became the richest and most powerful man to have ever lived.

> *If any of you lack wisdom, let him ask of God, that given to all men liberally, and upbraiding not; and it shall be given him.*

> **James 1:5**

Being of a sound mind gives us the *intelligence* to challenge the things that are not lining up with God's word and will. God wants us to have the ability to see the enemy's attack so that we know how to pray, intercede, and approach His thrown with our petitions. If we see something that is out of line then we can cry Abbas Father. If we are suffering injustice, we can run to our Father and tell him our concerns and seek guidance. A sound mind is exactly what the enemy does ***not*** want us to have. It's like the bully that wants to pick on the smaller, weaker, slower child in school. That child will have two minds. Should I run; should I cry for help; should I attempt to fight; or should I just give in? The enemy can destroy a person not with this type of thinking, but with their inability to think correctly.

So we have not been given the spirit of fear by our Father. It is Satan that wants to force this type of spirit into us. We should resist anything that anyone is trying to force into or onto us that has not been approved by our Father. A sound mind will rise up and remind us that this is not what we have been taught. What our Father has given us are the components; the tools to grow in His grace and be like Him. Our Father has given us three components to stand strong and confident: Power, Love, and a Sound Mind. What child does not want to grow up and have the same attributes and characteristics of a good Father?

If you insist on being a disobedient child; if you want to play around on the enemy's playground and do not like the truth of what you are hearing, then please feel free to cover your ears.

Notes And Reflections For The Reader:

Notes And Reflections For The Reader:

Suffering for the Faith

Finish the Fight like a Champion!

"I have fought a good fight, I have finished [my] course; I have kept the faith:"

2 Timothy 4:7

There is no nice way to put this. It hurts in all parts of your being. It feels like your mind has left you; like your spirit is crushed; and your body will not allow you to stand straight and throw one more punch. Like the character Noe said, in one of my favorite movies, 'The Matrix', *"It feels like dying!"*

I have no idea why God allows this type of suffering in our lives. If I had to guess, I would say that in His plans, He always has a plan that extends into our present future which will transition into our *eternal* future. There are things that He wants to bring out of us. There is potential that lies dormant and, as yet, is untapped. He has designed us to be able to withstand a lot more than we know ourselves. If God does not allow us to suffer, then it might never become a realization and it would stay hidden.

It is like a sword maker; the fire has to be hot enough to first melt the iron ore. Then the iron ore has to be removed from the fire and shaped. It is shaped while it is still red hot; it is beaten and twisted and stretched during this time. Then it is reheated and beaten and twisted and stretched some more.

The iron must go through this process for hours before the sword maker can achieve the desired result. When the sword is near completion, it must be cooled down and then reheated yet again to place any distinguishing marks in the metal. This is called Me-Kiri. This requires a heavy hammer and a chisel shaped object with a blade that can score metal. The sword is again beaten; and again we see the pressure change during the carving of the sword.

There are far too many steps in the Japanese sword making process to mention in this study. Rest assured that the finished product is the strongest sword on the planet.

Suffering for what you believe is the mark that those who have been remembered in history have done and gone through just this type of shaping process. It is ***why*** they are remembered! It requires dedication to what you believe that surpasses what anyone else might consider rational. It makes a statement that echoes through time and screams <u>*change*</u>. It is the voice of a man crying, "Repent, for the 'Kingdom' is at hand!" in the wilderness. It is the expedition that took a man (Hannibal) over mountains on elephant back and the voice of a man who spent twenty seven years in prison (Nelson Mandela) and was freed only to later become president of that same country. It is the voices of men that sailed halfway around the world to find a new horizon and found a new country that no one else believed could exist. Suffering is the voice of the triumphant against everything that is standing in their way and saying that it can ***not*** be done.

Suffering for your beliefs dares the person behind you to follow in your footsteps. It challenges those that have never taken chances; who would have never thought to reach for the goals that were considered unreachable. It is something that is inside of you and that forces you to endure the hurt and anguish so that your belief can give someone else a choice and a chance that you were not afforded; or that they were not offered.

It does not say that others must believe what you believe, but it places more than one option on the table. When they can see how deeply committed you are, it will inspire within them courage and bravery. It will inspire the idea that things have the potential to be different.

The price is definitely self, but sometimes it is life! Many have paid it willingly; this is how deep their convictions were and are! How much more should we strive to find something, in this short life, that we can hold onto with both hands and believe with everything in us; with our entire being? It becomes a little easier when the pioneer, of what we choose to believe, has suffered and paid the ultimate price for that belief.

Jesus could have given up at any time. He could have chosen a different path with a different outcome. He could have made different decisions and ruled instead of served, but He chose the road less taken. He suffered for what He believed; for what He had faith in; humanity. He showed the entire world what having faith and believing in something can achieve. His name has outlasted history itself; this is why the calendar is B.C. (Before Christ) and A.D. (Anu Dominic – The Year of Our Lord). Making this great of an impact should speak volumes to us about what one man's belief and faith can accomplish. [He was, however God incarnate]

Nevertheless, He was our example of how suffering for the faith can obtain an eternal benefit. I teach this as well to the youth as a thought provoker. The title of the lesson is: *"Who Would Die for a Lie?"* The lesson goes through all of the claims that try to expel Christ's resurrection and ascension. Why bury the truth in history's annals? This is a beautiful and glorious thing! His life and miracles are a matter of historic fact. His resurrection and ascension were witnessed by more than five hundred people. The evidence of the stories in scripture are still being discovered to be *true* in every culture worldwide. The death of Jesus' disciples is a matter of historic record. They were shot through with arrows, decapitated, crucified upside down, stoned, boiled and left to die in prison for their faith. My question to my students is always the title of the lesson, *"Who would die for a lie?"* The only thing that the disciples had to do was recant and walk away. They chose to suffer and die for their faith!

We really do not have to look back two thousand years in order to find this type of commitment. Africans are suffering for Christianity today on a continent that is predominantly Muslim. Chinese and Japanese alike are suffering for daring to step outside of their traditional belief systems to hold onto Christianity. Hindus are losing family and friends for proclaiming the Christian faith. Others are losing their lives in a more 'modern' fashion that could not be used in antiquity.

Even before the disciples were killed for their belief, Paul suffered for Christ. He suffered, but yet he pressed on and pressed through.

So my final question to you Dear Reader is, "Are you willing to suffer for the Faith?" This is my third book on the subject of Spiritual Warfare and I pray that it will not be my last! The experience that God requires for me to pen this topic is literally killing me. I will end this particular portion by outlining Paul's dissertation and Peter's synopsis on suffering for the faith.

> *"Seeing that many glory after the flesh, I will glory also. For ye suffer fools gladly, seeing ye [yourselves] are wise. For ye suffer, if a man bring you into bondage, if a man devour [you], if a man take [of you], if a man exalt himself, if a man smite you on the face. I speak as concerning reproach, as though we had been weak. Howbeit wherein soever any is bold, (I speak foolishly,) I am bold also. Are they Hebrews? so [am] I. Are they Israelites? so [am] I. Are they the seed of Abraham? so [am] I. Are they ministers of Christ? (I speak as a fool) I [am] more; in labors more abundant, in stripes above measure, in prisons more frequent, in deaths oft. Of the Jews five times received I forty [stripes] save one. Thrice was I beaten with rods, once was I stoned, thrice I suffered shipwreck, a night and a day I have been in the deep; [In] journeying often, [in] perils of waters, [in] perils of robbers, [in] perils by [mine own] countrymen, [in] perils by the heathen, [in] perils in the city, [in] perils in the wilderness, [in] perils in the sea, [in] perils among false brethren; In weariness and painfulness, in watching often, in hunger and thirst, in fasting often, in cold and nakedness. Beside those things that are without, that which cometh upon me daily, the care of all the churches. Who is weak, and <u>I am not weak?</u> who is offended, and I burn not? If I must needs glory, I will glory of the things which concern mine infirmities."*

> 2 Corinthians 11:18-**30**

1 Peter 4:16 *Yet if [any man suffer] as a Christian, <u>let him not be ashamed</u>; but let him glorify God on this behalf.*

1 Peter 4:17 *For the time [is come] that judgment must begin at the house of God: and if [it] first [begin] at us, what shall the end [be] of them that obey not the gospel of God?*

1 Peter 4:18 *And if the righteous scarcely be saved, where shall the ungodly and the sinner appear?*

1 Peter 4:19 *Wherefore let them that suffer according to the will of God commit the keeping of their souls [to him] in well doing, <u>as unto a faithful Creator</u>.*

I'll say it the way that scripture says it when we suffer, "*Man-Up and act like a man!*" (*Quit yourselves like men!*)

> *"Be strong, and <u>quit yourselves like men</u>, O ye Philistines, that ye be not servants unto the Hebrews, as they have been to you: quit yourselves like men, and <u>fight</u>."*

1 Samuel 4:9

> *"Watch ye, stand fast in the faith, quit you like men, be strong."*

1 Corinthians 16:13

Notes And Reflections For The Reader:

Notes And Reflections For The Reader:

Favor With God and With Men

It had to be God!

"And the angel came in unto her (Mary), and said, Hail, [thou that art] highly favoured, the Lord [is] with thee: blessed [art] thou among women. And when she saw [him], she was troubled at his saying, and cast in her mind what manner of salutation this should be."

Luke 1:28, **29**

I have noticed in scripture that often times we pray and we *do* believe that God hears us, but we are not prepared for Him to answer. The belief portion is what turns His ears toward us and makes Him desire to move. Remember, His answer is always Yes, No, or Wait, but *faith* is the key to getting any response at all.

In the Old Testament, God's angels would show up with messages that caused His servants to wonder about the favor that they were receiving from God. They were in disbelief about the fact that God thought so highly of them; then they questioned *themselves* and their own capabilities. Remember this Dear Reader; if God calls you, He has already given you the ability and the victory. Our righteousness and justification is *through* and *in* Christ, so all of our thinking and the apprehension that we are doing is counter productive to our beginning to *move* with and in *His* calling.

When the angel appeared to Gideon, he was hiding from the Michiganite, behind a wine press, so that he could gather wheat. When the angel addressed him as a 'mighty man of valor', Gideon

126

doubted. He asked the angel where God was and where were God's miracles in the time of his county's trouble?

> *"And there came an angel of the LORD, and sat under an oak which [was] in Oprah, that [pertained] unto Josh the Anchorite: and his son Gideon threshed wheat by the wine press, to hide [it] from the Michiganite. And the angel of the LORD appeared unto him, and said unto him, The LORD [is] with thee, <u>thou mighty man of valor.</u> And Gideon said unto him, Oh my Lord, if the LORD be with us, why then is all this befallen us? and where [be] all his miracles which our fathers told us of, saying, Did not the LORD bring us up from Egypt? but now the LORD hath forsaken us, and delivered us into the hands of the Michiganite. And the LORD looked upon him, and said, <u>Go in this thy might, and thou shalt save Israel from the hand of the Michiganite: have not I sent thee?"</u>*

Judges 6:11-14

Notice that the angel did not answer Gideon questions, but the angel allowed God to answer Gideon Himself. God basically told Gideon to do what He had called him to do and then asked a question: *"Aren't I God? I am the one sending <u>you</u> to save Israel!"*

Gideon passion for His people and his recognition of God stirred God to move on Israel's behalf. Gideon was not prepared to hear that he was considered to be fearless and heroic by GOD! He sure did not know that he had found favor with God to the extent that God was willing to use him in this fashion.

<u>VALOR</u> means: *Heroic, Fearless, and Brave, having Nerve, Spirit and Gallantry.*

This had to be an awesome feeling once Gideon realized that God had a purpose for his life!

"And the angel said unto her, Fear not, Mary: for thou hast found favour with God."

Luke 1:30

Mary was a young girl, perhaps still in her teens when Gabriel appeared to her. Of course she was surprised by the angel's greeting. She wondered what type of greeting that it was and how she could have found *favor* with God.

The dye was already cast and the plan was in motion. The only thing that Mary had to do was believe and continue doing what she had already been doing. Joseph was in place and Jesus was on His way. Joseph had already found favor with God as well because he was in place and in position to raise, teach, and take care of Jesus. God chose a man that would not look down on Mary or slander her name. He chose a man that would not divorce or embarrass her. He chose a man with a good profession and one that would protect Jesus.

God chose two people that He could trust to raise and take care of Jesus (His only son) correctly. Both Joseph and Mary found favor with God and with man. Mary only wondered what the angel wanted with a young lady like herself when he appeared, but she believed. Joseph had a similar visitation and he also trusted and believed.

Finding favor with both man and God can be difficult; nearly impossible, but it can happen. When our thinking lines up with God's thinking, the scripture says that even our enemies will be at peace with us.

"When a man's ways please the LORD, he maketh even his enemies to be at peace with him".

Proverbs 16:7

God's will and His ways will cause our enemies to recognize God in us. They may be in rebellion against God, but that part of God that remains in them; His image and His likeness will always cry out from the inside of them to its creator. It will cry out even when they have seared their conscience and gotten onto the wrong path. Only those that have gone as far as to invite God's enemy into their lives stand outside of, and without the possibility of having the capacity to return to His presence. God is longsuffering, but there does come a time when He will give man over to a *reprobate* mind. There comes a time when He will harden a person's heart ire. allow what is already in them to come out.

We can find favor with God by being obedient to His will and by continuing to acknowledge Him for whom He is and what He does for us daily. This will cause, even those who do not believe what we believe, to be respectful of *what* we believe and *who* we are serving. They will be able to see us as examples of what God's people are like and recognize that we are a breed apart; that we are not following the world. This speaks volumes without us ever having to brow beat people with the 'gospel'. We have to settle in our minds that the only way that they can come to Christ anyway is if the Spirit of God has drawn them. Christians that try to force the gospel message down the throats of sinners are usually rejected and do more damage than good to the 'Kingdom'. This is difficult because once we have found the good news of Christ and have set our feet on the right path; it is definitely hard to keep quiet. It is news that cannot be withheld or contained. It takes time to minister the gospel in a way that people will willingly receive it.

In previous times, the gospel was accepted wholeheartedly and it attracted everyone who had not previously heard it. Today it has been so watered down and conjoined with so many negative things in this world; it has now become more difficult to minister. Of course, this is also a part of the enemy's plan. He also knows that a little leaven Leavenworth the whole lump. This is shocking because of the fact that it is the greatest free gift that has ever been offered. My opinion is that if we live in a world that has become so sinful that we cannot give away a *free* gift, then we are truly living in bad times.

> **"And Jesus increased in wisdom and stature, and in favour with God and man."**

> Luke 2:52

During man's natural lifespan, *some* things will follow the natural pattern of life's course. We will grow in the way that God has designed the human body to grow. We will also learn and be taught as a normal part of growing up and maturing.

Jesus learned as a corporeal man and He grew in size as a natural man and He learned as a young man. The **example** was that He grew in favor with God <u>first</u> and with mankind <u>second</u>. He set forth this example as the *best* way to proceed in life. Everyone will not accomplish the first two portions of Jesus' example because of time and chance. Favor with God has to come as a matter of belief and Godly reverence. The favor with man part will come as the world is able to associate our real belief and reverence for God and see it in us.

> **"Praising God, and having favour with all the people. And the Lord added to the church daily such as should be saved."**

> Act 2:47

We see again that doing God's will gives us His favor. Scripture tells us in Psalm 22:3 that God inhabits the praises of His people. God was pleased with the church that was forming after Pentecost and He added more people *daily* as would believe in His son. The disciples and new converts praised God and had favor with all people so God blessed them. God's blessings always follow His recognition and acknowledgment and afford us His favor.

We also see that being obedient and the identification of God will cause Him to change our situation as well as elevate us to a different level in life. God can and will work with a son or daughter that is obedient. God will also allow people to perceive us in a different way. Whereas they would have formed preconceived notions about who we are and question our abilities, but God will change their perspective.

"And delivered him out of all his afflictions, and gave him favour and wisdom in the sight of Pharaoh King of Egypt; and he made him governor over Egypt and all his house."

Acts 7:10

Joseph had no experience in government or in the type of leadership required to execute any sort of rule over a foreign dignitary's whole cabinet. Joseph is a prime example of God's giving us favor, in the world, because of our obedience and recognition of Him. Joseph held onto his faith in God and graduated from *prisoner* to *vice president* (Sounds a lot like the Nelson Mandela story). God's favor delivered him from his circumstances and elevated him before others who had more skill and experience than he did. Pharaoh's perception was changed as God's blessings rained down upon Joseph. Joseph was blessed and through him the ruler of Egypt and his people were blessed.

Favor with God is multidimensional. If we can find favor with God then He will extend those blessings to those around us. This is another way that God's Spirit draws people to His Son.

They will get blessed through our walk and say, *"There must be something to all of this Jesus stuff?"*

Notes And Reflections For The Reader:

Notes And Reflections For The Reader:

More Is Required

Men Want More Than God

"But he that knew not, and did commit things worthy of stripes, shall be beaten with few [stripes]. For unto whomsoever much is given, of him shall be much required: and <u>to whom men have committed much, of him they will ask the more</u>."

Luke 12:48

There is always accountability! We may try to erase it from the equation or bury it in our minds, but this does *not* change the reality that the facts still remain the **_facts_**! We are always accountable for what we know and for our actions, whether we want to acknowledge this or not. Knowledge *is* power and either you are using it correctly or you are misusing it. The problem comes in when people listen to your misdirection or your error in perception. They are now are at risk because you have acquired the knowledge and you are not sharing it correctly or at all.

When you have knowledge and it is not divulged appropriately; when it is held and not dissimulated, you do a disservice to your self and to others. Knowledge expressed at the proper time, place and fashion may save someone's life. If a new employee is not given the appropriate direction and protocol for the correct response during a fire, then how will they escape, help save others or survive themselves?

"No man, <u>when he hath lighted a candle</u>, putteth [it] in a secret place, neither under a bushel, but on a candlestick, that they which come in may see the light."

Luke 11:33

The light is *knowledge*! When we have acquired knowledge it is meant to be shared and given to everyone so that others can have, at the very least, the benefit of being informed. It is never meant to be hidden or held, but revealed and shown like the light of a candle. When we come someone that is a member of any organization that requires 'levels' or anything that calls for us to ascend in order to get to the truth, then that is a form of witchcraft. People these days claim to be in what is commonly called the 'Illuminati'/ 'order of perfectionists' or join 'freemasonry' which is a similar form. These groups are controlled by men who are deceived and being allowed to think that they are in control and pulling the strings. In actuality, if we were the ones that were truly in control, we would allow the ones seeking position to believe exactly that. They would always believe that they were achieving greater and greater knowledge with each step, but would never get to where the men who are actually pulling the strings sit. Satan and his angels do a far better job than man. This is a deception where Satan uses men against men to achieve his goals and objectives.

As a people that have been given the greatest gift that humanity has ever known; we owe a debt to mankind to make sure that we share the good news and our eternal fortune.

> *Now to him that is of power to establish you according to my gospel, and the preaching of Jesus Christ, according to the revelation of the mystery, which was kept secret since the world began.*

Romans 16:25

> *And for me, that utterance may be give unto me, that I may open my mouth boldly, to make known the mystery of the gospel.*

Ephesians 6:19

The good news of God sending humanity a Savior was never meant to be kept a secret. God has desired for His plans to be made accessible to everyone on planet earth. Since God has offered us so much through His Son Jesus, we have an accountability factor that really cannot be overlooked or dismissed. How can we expect so great a gift without there being any expectation on our part? What has always struck me as incredible about the particular scripture Luke 12:48 is the fact that men will require more from you than God will. God has His requirements and He should because He's God. It is easy to understand that if someone is given a great deal, a great deal will be expected of them, but for man to require more is startling.

Think about it, when you do something for someone, they will look at you a lot differently than God. God looks at us from the perspective of knowing more about you than you know about yourself. He looks at you from the standpoint of **knowledge**; from the standpoint of knowing how and why He created you. Man will always look at us from the standpoint of what we can do for him/her. Even in marriage sad to say, that is worldly today's standpoint as opposed to *God-Centered* the way it was intended. There is the selfish factor of each person feeling as if they will benefit in some way from the other. In today's society, people are not marrying solely for *love.* Marriage has become a business arrangement or an arrangement for convenience.

God has His requirements for mankind and they are absent from the carnal idealistic of men. God's requisites for us embody only those things that can be accounted *reasonable* and *just* for a Creator and Father. Man's requirements only mimic Gods and always go far beyond what we are able to perform and/or deliver. God's requirements are for *our* best, while man's requirements are for *man's* best. God's requirements are for *our* ultimate development and improvement, while man's requirements are for man's success and accomplishment only.

The similarity lies in the fact that the punishment for not meeting the prerequisites of either bears a resemblance. For both sides the punishment is according to knowledge. Man will look at a situation and desire a certain justification. The saying is that the punishment should fit the crime. God feels the same way, but He is approaching it from a different perspective. He is approaching any infraction from the standpoint of love and the desire for a closer relationship with us. Included in that is ***grace*** (blessing us with what we have not earned or deserve) and ***mercy*** (not accounting to us what we actually do deserve and have coming). Man's punishment is based on what man has viewed as a deficit in his own plans and/or worldview.

We all have our own viewpoint and even our own ideas about how to progress in life. Some people make decisions that will allow them to be in position for success in the world. Others will take the road less traveled and can also achieve their goals in life. What I would like to convey Dear Reader is that if we align our will with God's will, then the journey could be so much easier. There will still be bumps in the road; there will still be tests to pass; and there will still be adversity that must be overcome. There will still be instances where we are at a crossroads, but isn't easier to be able to turn to someone that knows? Isn't easier to be able to turn to someone that has the power to get us through our difficult times and always has our best interest at heart? I do believe that when we take the view point that those things are man's prerequisites and these are God's; the odds will shift in our favor when we choose God's.

To whom much is given, much is required. What should always be taken into consideration is the ***one*** doing the giving!

Notes And Reflections For The Reader:

Notes And Reflections For The Reader:

The Cares of
This World

The World Doesn't Care for You!

Falling in love with this world will end in heartbreak every single time. That does not seem fair does it? Could it possibly *ever* be fair? A person will do everything that the world requires and find out that the world has used them up and left them for the next lover. This love affair requires all of your time; it requires all of your energy; it requires your self esteem and your dignity; in short it requires the best part of you, your *youth*.

Think about Howard Hughes; there wasn't much that he didn't have and yet he died like someone who had given himself and his vitality fully to the world that he thought loved him. From an outside standpoint many of us would have traded places with him thinking that we would have done things differently. He had an uncanny business sense and enough money to make his dreams a reality. His passion was airplanes and he became a juggernaut in the aerodynamics industry, but this goal cost him his peace and sound mind. Women, dinner parties, servants, and all of the money he could spend could not satisfy the pull that the world had on his mind. He was continuously driven to outdo what he had previously accomplished. His drive to make a name for himself and to be the best in his field caused him to spend his final years as a recluse. The aeronautics industry has changed drastically due, in large part, to the accomplishments of Howard Hughes. Now that the world had what if needed, what was the need for Howard Hughes?

It may sound strange to look at it from this standpoint, but why wouldn't we think of these things from this viewpoint? We speak in terms of '*mother earth*' and say things like, "*That 70's spirit…*" Why wouldn't we give the 'world' a human persona; the quality of having people *love* it? If we can look at it from this perspective, then we can grant it the ability to accept or reject what we are putting into it; the *way* that we love it.

Make no mistake; loving the things that this world has to offer is far less beneficially than you will be led to believe.

What you will see is someone that is at the pinnacle their personal glory; the height of where man can be elevated and therein is the attraction for everyone else that will follow. Professional athletes prove this on a regular basis. It is just a matter of turning on the T.V.

I remember wanting to be like O.J. Simpson as a young man; I even had his football jersey. His demise was followed worldwide by the media and followed by still incident after incident. His football career was over; his wife and her boyfriend were dead; and his lifelong success and glory were erased by the very world that once loved him.

Michael Jackson, Elvis Presley and Whitney Houston have very similar stories. It is too easy for us to sit back and speak about how things could have been different. It is too easy for us to comment on the different road that *we* would have taken, if given the same opportunities. The world, that loved and idolized the 'King of Pop' but, later villainous him as a child molester. The same world that loved 'The King' made millions off of his drug induced overdose and his wealth. The world made millions by watching her and her husband in a drug induced relationship on national television. They watched her lose her God given multifaceted voice. These three people were acclaimed to be forerunners and trailblazers in the music industry until the world had finished implementing its own standards and they had outlived their usefulness.

What the 'world' will not tell you is that many of those who have achieved unbelievable heights and fame have 'loved' the Gods of this world rather than the God that created it. Russell Simmons, Kimono Lee, Michael Jackson, Oozy Osborne, Marilyn Manson, The Beatles, Jim Hendricks, Janice Joplin and many, many others have sold their souls to the 'gods' of this world for fame and fortune. Very few of them are still alive, but you can research their lifestyle and mentality very easily.

The world will take its toll on those that love it and the price is always too high to pay. One of the main problems is that loving the world, or the gods that are behind the scenes, is in direct opposition with the One True God.

> *"Ye adulterers and adulteresses know ye not that the <u>friendship of the world is enmity with God</u>? Whosoever therefore will be a friend of the world is the enemy of God."*

James 4:4

> *"Because <u>the carnal mind [is] enmity against God</u>: for it is not subject to the law of God, neither indeed can be."*

Romans 8:7

> *"<u>Love not the world, neither the things [that are] in the world. If any man love the world, the love of the Father is not in him.</u>"*

1 John 2:15

> *"If ye were of the world, the world would love his own: but because ye are not of the world, but I have chosen you out of the world, <u>therefore the world hater you.</u>"*

John 15:19

Make no errors about how you look at this subject. The world has a *persona*; whether it is the 'spirit' that is governing the age or the mentality that the general populace has, this is a love/hate relationship. The scripture says in Matthew 6:24 & Luke 16:13 that you cannot serve two masters, because you will **love** only one and you will **hate** the other one. God will not be anyone's second. He requires the number one spot and He will take offense to anyone or anything that seeks to fill it. It's like trying to work two jobs. You can love both jobs, but eventually you will burn out and begin to despise the job that *you* feel has the least benefits even though they both have the same duties. You can despise the other job because you do not like your coworkers or the supervisor.

We have all seen people that tend to get their priorities backward. They esteem the weekend higher than the week. They look forward to the weekend because of the Friday night partying; Saturday because of the ability to sleep in and party Saturday night; and Sunday because they have a chance to be in church around people that will pray for their Friday and Saturday. (Hope I didn't step on anyone's toes?) The priority is backward because the work week is what allows for any of the previous activities. The work week is what sustains the quality and standard of life, so enjoying what the world has to offer has its place. A night of bowling or a night of dinner and jazz is completely acceptable in God's sight; I am reasonably sure that God likes Jazz or at least good music.

Look back at chapter 2, **Don Lucifero**. What happens is that Satan will pervert the thinking that would normally put the priorities into the right order. If I do this first, I can still do that and have fun. Prioritizing the wrong one will most certainly mean the loss of or inability to do either. I have had friends that have called into work drunk or were too tired from a party to show up on time. I have friends that abuse their sick leave and personal leave to the point of not being dependable to their boss and eventually get fired. Still others show up to work five or ten minutes late until it becomes recognized and a cause for chastisement and then termination. These might seem like very small things, but think about it, in Eden, Satan only inserted a three letter word and that messed up all of humanity.

> *But of the tree of the knowledge of good and evil, thou shalt not eat of it: for in the day that thou eatest thereof <u>thou shalt surely die.</u>*

> **Genesis 2:17**

> ### *And the serpent said unto the woman, <u>Ye shall not surely die:</u>*

> **Genesis 3:4**

God has told us why humanity is in the situation that it is in and He expects for His children to listen. Adam surrendered the deed and title to earth in Eden and so of course Satan is going to make the world, that he is presently running, seem like one big party. Satan will misdirect us so that we will focus on anything and everything but God. He will make it so tantalizing and attractive that we will find it hard to resist. He will compare the things of God to his own pleasures and make God's directives to man look restrictive and confining. This is a backward way of thinking when we realize that God has created everything that we have and will have in heaven and on earth. Satan is taking something that he did not create and making it appear to be *his* invention; *his* idea. Remember, we haven't even seen heaven yet!

If you ever get the impression that Christianity is boring; too confining or too restrictive, then ask yourself how much you are putting into it. Are you praising God and throwing up your hands like you were at a Jay-Z concert? Are you dancing at Christian events as hard as you do at a nightclub? Are you having as much fun interacting with your brothers and sisters in Christ at the church picnic the same as you would at the bar or casino? Ask yourself, *"Why is Satan so much fun?" "Why does the world seem to be more attractive than the eternal promise of heaven?"*

I can assure you that God loves you and has a plan for you. He is waiting for you to RSVP the invitation that He sent by way of His Son. All you have to do is say yes and He will send someone to get you when the doors open. He will even provide the food and new clothes. Once you accept Christ and believe, then the place setting will be printed and set.

> **"And he saith unto me, Write, Blessed [are] they which are called unto the <u>marriage supper </u>of the Lamb. And he saith unto me, These are the true sayings of God."**

> Revelation 19:9

"He that overcome, <u>the same shall be clothed in white raiment</u>; and I will not blot out his name out of the book of life, but I will confess his name before my Father, and before his angels."

Revelation 3:5

Notes And Reflections For The Reader:

Notes And Reflections For The Reader:

Unmasked

What's In You Will Come Out Of You

"Because that, when they knew God, they glorified [him] not as God, <u>neither were thankful</u>; but became vain in their imaginations, and their foolish heart was darkened."

Romans 1:21

Guess what? A *Thank You* can go a long way; further than you may think! If I do the smallest thing for you like hold the door or allow you to pull your car in front of mine, I expect a *"thank you"* at the least. I will even take, "Thanks." This is a term of recognition for the smallest effort that you put forth. It is the acknowledgment of ones endeavor to make your life that much easier. How do we think that God should feel when we are not *thankful* and He is GOD?

This scripture is not speaking of the supposed person that has never heard the 'good news' of Jesus the Savior. This scripture is saying that these people have known God and are not giving Him the recognition that He deserves. After all, He did create the air that they breathe everyday for free. He does wake them up morning after morning. God is asking for a *thank you* and the recognition of who He is and what He can do and has already done.

On top of the fact that these people knew God (past tense); and did not glorify Him **as** God and also were not thankful; God *allowed* their foolish hearts to be darkened. God did not darken their hearts; He only allowed what was *in* them to come *out* of them. This is what He did with Pharaoh the King of Egypt.

When this happens, it is only God taking a step back and letting them have their way. It is God not interfering with man's freewill. As I have mentioned before, God has already revealed in His Word that we have an enemy. He has given us the choice; the freewill to choose His way. When we have our mind set on doing things our own way, then He will say, "Yes! Have it your way." It is at this point that the enemy will attack in full force and assault your mind. Satan's objective is to drag as many people to hell as he can and he doesn't mind using you or me to do it. The scripture says that 'when' they knew God, they did not glorify Him as God. They then become vain in their imaginations. This means: hopeless, unproductive, unsuccessful, useless, futile and worthless. This is hard for me to imagine as far as someone's thinking pattern is concerned. To fail at certain things is a point of life; it is a fact. To become useless in all that you imagine or futile in everything that you think is beyond me. The positive thoughts are now being mixed with negative ones. The ideas that could benefit you will now hinder you. Your natural attraction and magnetism with people is now placing the wrong people in your circle. Your gifts and talents are now being used in the wrong places and at the wrong times. What could be success is now destined for failure and so on. I will not place the entirety of what Paul finishes with, but please take the time to read verses 22-32 before you continue. Satan is a master at his game which is why we have to master ours.

Satan has seen that you have not recognized God and he wants to capitalize on it. He will take the fact that God has been insulted and removed your hedge of protection as the go ahead to destroy you.

A foolishly darkened heart is the least of your worries if God is not recognized and He steps away from you. We can find ourselves on a part of the road that we never knew existed. There is no light on this part of the road; there are no street signs; there don't appear to be any lanes marked and the other cars are driving a lot faster than what we *know* is the speed limit.

What is in you is not a matter of God's doing. He has already given you His image and His likeness upon conception. The ability to choose Him is already within you as a matter of freewill. God's Word tells us that creation itself speaks of a Creator without anyone having to be told. So the problem comes down to who is in your ear? With Eve, it was Satan that was in her ear. With Cain, it was also Satan, but with a slightly different approach. After injecting sin into the equation, Satan's work becomes easier. The sin nature is now inborn with mankind because of Adam and Eve's disobedience to God. Because, when they knew God, they did not glorify Him as God or remember to thank Him. Satan's work becomes easy when he has something in us that is working for him.

The sin nature in us is always fighting God and wanting to pull away from or coming into obedience and submission to Him. It is this nature in man that is actually hostile toward God. This is the single thing that has been injected into our beings that is forever trying to break away from God. It is trying to take the lead before our minds and control our spirits. Obedience to God is the last thing that the fleshly, worldly sin nature wants. This is why when God knocks on the door of our hearts; we should invite Him to come in. The knocking should prompt you to understand and realize that God will not force Himself upon us. God is a gentleman and He will wait for our invitation. If we choose not to open the door then that is a completely different story.

We already know that man is now born with a sin nature so did your parents seek God and point the way for you? Was there anyone that prayed fro you when they saw you going in the wrong direction? Have you realized that you have a need for a Savior? If none of these things apply to you, then the likelihood is that you have adopted a worldly survival technique. The things that a sin nature will allow to grow in you will always be struggling to break free and be in control. Look at scripture and the different listings and categorizing of sins and see how broad a topic this is. If we do not want to be controlled by sin; if we do not want what is innately in us to come out of us, then we need a restraint.

> *For the mystery of iniquity doth already work: only <u>he who now letterer [will let]</u>, until he be taken out of the way.*

2 Thessalonians 2:7

Paul is telling the Thessalonians that the mystery of sin is already at work. It is only God's Holy Spirit that is restraining it, but He will be taken out of the way at some point. Dear Readers, I have already seen far more in this world than I have wanted too; I pray that we all will be in the 'Kingdom' when the Holy Spirit of God is taken out of the earth. He is still in the earth restraining sin from completely taking hold of humanity; imagine if He takes His hands completely off and lets what is in man come out? We are already living in a time where we can see that He is loosening His grip and allowing more and more as man's foolish heart is being darkened. What will be the next vain imagination that we will be witness too before we are once again living in the days of Noah? There will be no flood this time; this time it will be a lot worse than Sodom and Gomorrah.

"But the heavens and the earth, which are now, by the same word are kept in store, reserved unto fire against the day of judgment and perdition of ungodly men."

2 Peter 3:7

When the spirit of God is taken completely out of the earth there will be chaos. Man is already challenging God and giving in to sin. It is like the desire to fight for righteousness has vanished. Man has a, *"let's try it"* attitude"; that is leading to a, *"he/she got away with it* **or** *is doing it"* attitude; that is leading to an *"I don't care"* attitude that is leading us straight to hell! This world is catching on fire one with every new thought, advance in technology, latest trend or style and every new pop star. Someone has to wake up and smell the flames.

What I would love to see in my lifetime is a true revival. I would like to see people in recognition of the fact that things cannot go along the way that they have. I would like to see the Biblical End Time prophecies being paid attention too. I would like to see someone take a stand the way that they did when I was growing up. Just one familiar face on the television that says, *"This isn't right."* I do not want it to be a televangelist either. Satan has made the majority of them laughing stocks or unbelievable at best. I would like to see someone like Bill Mather to have an epiphany and realize that he is now sitting in Saul's former position (Before he became the Apostle Paul) where he was persecuting and killing Christians. I would like to see the realization and love of Christ touch him to the point that he recants all of his previous pot-shots at the gospel of Christ. The saddest part about this comedic/ actor is that he is Jewish. Bill Mather has now been unmasked. Read his bio online and you may begin to understand why he hates God so much.

God says in His Word in the book of Exodus, *"This people is a stiff-necked people!"* He wanted to wipe the Jews off of the planet and start again with Moses. He had already done so much for them and had shown them the awesome power of His love. Imagine the people that God chose to be ***His*** people are the ones causing Him the most trouble.

What is in you will surely come out of you!

Notes And Reflections For The Reader:

Notes And Reflections For The Reader:

Home Sweet Home

What Country Do You Seek?

Where would you like to spend your vacation? When I go on vacation, there are two things that I desire above anything else. The first is that I will have peace of mind. The second is that I will be able to rest. If I can obtain *peace of mind*, then I have no doubt that rest will come easily. In my travels abroad, or even travels within the country, I have always required time where I would be able to think undisturbed and a comfortable place to rest with which I could end my day.

In my younger days it was easy to accept the gospel message, but Satan began to work on me around the age of thirteen. He began to burden me and pull on me with the cares of this world. It wasn't anything extraordinary, but he began to draw my attention to other things. I began to see girls differently, I began to get into sports and I began to hang around the wrong people. After graduation, I went to Howard University in Washington D.C. and I was truly out on my own. I was not under the umbrella of protection provided by living in a God fearing house; at least not to the degree that my accountability was being retained in the forefront of my thinking. I know now that I have a God that affords more *grace* and *mercy* than we can ever understand and a praying mother to thank for my re-entrance into the sheepfold. I had to experience a great deal before I began to recognize that I needed to repent and turn around.

It was when I began to seek God as an adult that my life began to do a 180^0. I began to see in God's Word that believing in the *saving* power, of Christ's sacrifice, was the only definite way to acquire the peace that I was craving. I didn't have to do anything accept believe in what God was saying. Did I try other faiths? Yes! You might not believe how many and I gained quite a bit of knowledge during my time and studies while searching for God in all of the wrong places. It was a young Christian woman that was immovable in her faith that stopped me dead in my tracks. In conversation, I began to try and convince her that my way of thinking was right and she said something very simple to me that made me rethink everything! Lisa responded to my tirade by saying, *"What difference does it make?"* At that point I basically stopped talking and I began to ask myself that very question. *"What difference did what I was talking about make?"* None! This is what is known as the simplicity of the gospel. She was not in my face, I was in hers. She was not stepping on my toes; I was attempting to step on hers. I was trying to prove **what** and to what end?

I met my beautiful wife Tammy shortly after that and began to study the *real* Word of God on a regular basis. I realized that unlike other faiths, I did not have to reach up and try to touch God; He had already reached down to touch *me* through His Son. *THERE* was my **peace**! Now I'm not saying that you can accept Christ and sit on your butt; not at all. What I am saying is that my residence in heaven with my creator is not *based* on anything that I will have to *do* here on earth except say YES! My eternal vacation is not determined by my worldly works.

It was these scriptures that solidified things in my mind; helped me remember what I already knew.

> *"These all died in faith, <u>not having received the promises, but having seen them afar off, and were persuaded of [them], and embraced [them], and confessed that they were strangers and pilgrims on the earth.</u> For they that say such things declare plainly that they seek a <u>country</u>. And truly, if they had been mindful of that [<u>country</u>] from whence they came out, they might have had opportunity to have returned. But now they desire a better [<u>country</u>], that is, an heavenly: wherefore God is not ashamed to be called their God: for he hath prepared for them a city."*

> Hebrews 11:13-**16**

God's Word is truly correct when it tells us to, "*Raise a child in the way that he should go and when he is older he will not depart from it.*" I believe that everyone will spend their time in this 'country'; the world. The question is whether or not they will choose to stay in Egypt or look for the Exodus. We have to have our time in the world, for the purpose of being able to use our free will. This is so that we can exercise our freedom of 'choice'. God is righteous enough that He would never take a gift back or undo His creation without offering *grace* and *mercy* first.

These patriarchs all died persuaded of the promise of a gift that they did not receive here on earth. They all understood that the country, that they were in, was not the country in which they desired to stay. They looked forward to journeying to their *true* country and were not ashamed of their real citizenship while they were abroad. They were not ashamed to be called citizens of the 'Kingdom' and therefore God was not ashamed to be called their God. These people held onto their faith and claimed their real citizenship against every difficulty that they faced in the foreign country.

God calls people out of their current situation and awaits our response to His invitation to become a citizen of His country. Many times we have become so comfortable in the country that we are in, we will not entertain the idea of visiting God's country. Some people will do the research to find out what God's country is about and then visit. Others will decline to visit and choose to stay in the country where they are comfortable and never experience the blessings that God has in store for them. It all comes down to '*realization*'. Can you realize that there may be something better waiting for you someplace else? Do you desire something more than what you've grown accustomed too? The people that ask themselves this question will never be comfortable until they have found the answer. Their entire life is a search for what they know within themselves is their destiny or (I don't believe in this word, but I will use it...) *fate*! There is something that awaits them somewhere and they are living a life that presses toward that end.

This is what inspired the patriarchs in antiquity and what is still driving millions today. It is the **hope** that the promise of God is awaiting them in the not so distant future. We are looking for the country that God promised us and the new city in which we will live with Him in eternity.

The key to this scripture has always been an encouragement to me. It is the fact that, these all **died** '*in faith*' and did <u>not</u> receive the promise. They must have been 'persuaded' beyond doubt and without any possibility of being discouraged. This is a blessing in and of itself especially in a world where people simply do not believe in or trust anything anymore. They believed God throughout their entire lives and did *not* receive what God promised. This is dedication to what you believe in against all odds and against all persecution. To believe in something so deeply that you are willing to die not only with, but for that belief speaks devotion that you rarely find today. You may think that you have this type of dedication, but is what you are dedicated too real? Is your dedication eternal? Does the belief that you hold have the ability to change and/or improve your current lifestyle? If you are still comfortable in the country in which you reside; or if you cannot be distinguished from those around you without faith, then you have believed a lie. Somewhere, during the course of your existence, in your current country, you have been deceived.

There must be the ability to present the evidence of what you believe determinable in some place; in some way; somewhere. Many people will say that there is not enough evidence to prove that Jesus is the Messiah or that He was and is God incarnate. Is this true? There is more evidence to prove that He <u>was</u> and <u>is</u> who He claims to be than there is to disprove it. Too often doubters would like to dismiss the facts and never show enough evidence to prove their point. There is a world wide web of research that can now be done with new evidence being found constantly. This is a fact, so since this is true, why do we not rest in the hope of the promises of God?

If 95% of the world's population believes in a higher power, then it stands to reason that an intelligent man will not find himself in the bottom five percentile. All that a person has to do is search for the truth. The Word of God will ultimately speak for itself! Once God makes Himself known to you, then the invitation has been extended, stood and remained for two thousand years. We all know that death is an absolute reality for every man; this is our earthly house or tabernacle. God's promise and hope invites us to have a place in heaven with or creator for eternity.

> *"For we know that if our earthly house of [this] tabernacle were dissolved, we have a building of God, <u>an house not made with hands</u>, eternal in the heavens."*

2 Corinthians 5:1

> *"But Christ being come an high priest of good things to come, by <u>a greater and more perfect tabernacle</u>, not made with hands, that is to say, not of this building."*

Hebrews 9:11

God promises us a dwelling place in a new country where we will live in houses that have not been built with hands. This is our spiritual hope. The country that we are going to is a spiritual place where everything will be more perfect than where we are now. All we have to do is believe and spend a small portion of our time doing the research required to find out about this country and new 'Kingdom'. The citizenship requirements are not as detailed as we tend to think that they are and the retirement benefits are the best. I plan to be one of the people that hold onto the faith during the course of *my* life. I am definitely looking forward to God's promise. From what I read in the brochure, the country is beautiful!

Notes And Reflections For The Reader:

Notes And Reflections For The Reader:

The "This Is What I Want" Line

The Selfish Instead of Selfless Program

This line is getting longer and longer in these last days! It is actually unbelievable that so many people are willing to place their personal needs and desires before anyone else's. The world has already gravitated to Dog-Eat-Dog and there doesn't seem to be any return charity for the sake of charity. Even if the topic is the difference is between right and wrong, you may hear, *"I know, but that is not what I want!"*

This is a sad state of affairs because it doesn't consider the elderly, children, marriage, friendship, or your fellowman. The selfish mentality transcends all boundaries; all instances; and all situations. This mentality does not take the condition of others into consideration for even the slightest instance. The enemy has designed the negative response to needs to be a 'knee jerk' reaction. *"Can you? No, I'm sorry I can't!"* *"Will you? I would, but..."* *"I need... I'm in the same situation as you, but at any other time..."* The responses have already been programmed to countermand any query that will hinder this person's desires.

The primary motivator is *one* man's wants, desires, and perceived needs. Once the enemy has planted this particular kind of seed, it takes root in man's self preservation wiring. Over time it becomes hardwired and eventually a part of a person's system. Since God designed the system, He is the only one that can disconnect the wiring. This mentality, once hardwired, will run without ever having to be updated or modified. It will automatically adjust itself to be compatible with every other system that God has hardwired in us. It will override compassion; it will minimize the needs of others; it will attempt to file away 'love' and it will most definitely bypass any program that we attempt to open that does not upgrade the '*selfish*'.

Luke's gospel and letter to the Greeks paints a very accurate picture of the difference between these two types of mentalities.

> *"Two men went up into the temple to pray; the one a Pharisee, and the other a publican. The Pharisee stood and prayed thus <u>with himself</u>, God, I thank thee, that I am not as other men [are], extortioners, unjust, adulterers, or even as this publican. I fast twice in the week, I give tithes of all that I possess."*

Luke 18:10-**12**

THIS IS AN EXCERPT FROM BARNES AND NOBLES' COMMENTARY ON THE PHARISEE AND PUBLICAN:

Stood and prayed thus with himself - Some have proposed to render this, "stood by himself" and prayed. In this way it would be characteristic of the sect of the Pharisees, who dreaded the contact of others as polluting, and who were disposed to say to all, Stand by yourselves.

For further reading you may refer to the website below to read the complete article:

http://www.ccel.org/ccel/barnes/ntnotes.vi.xviii.xi.html?device= desktop

These types of people sit on the thrones of their own hearts; they cannot give God His rightful position because they pray too and worship themselves. It is very easy for selfish people to identify another's flaws; usually the ones that they point out mirror their own. A selfish person will always proclaim themselves to be giving people and wanting the benefit of others before they satisfy the yearnings of their own desires. This is a self deception. They will give what they have an excess of and never to the point where they lack anything. The selfish person will never admit that they have deprived anyone else. It is too hard for them to concede to the fact that they have injured their fellowman in their actions. Their perception of themselves is always as being '*good*' and within the _will_ of God. It is always easy for these people to compare themselves to those persons that are clearly not in God's will; like the Pharisee did. One of their biggest ways to vindicate themselves is by using the word '*people*'. They are right that 'people' do a lot of things and get themselves into all kinds of situations, but I have never met anyone named 'people'. It is another of the enemy's tricks – **misdirection**. Other people will never have anything to do with what God has called YOU and I to be.

> *"Because it is written, Be ye holy; for I am holy."*

1 Peter 1:16

This means that God has called us to be *different* and apart like He is *different*. The selfish person has the 'tree' mentality. This is how they seek to blend into the forest; by comparing themselves to the other trees. They do not wish to be different. What they want is the option to, "*Have their cake and eat it too.*" There is nothing Godly or different about this mentality as you can see from the scripture.

The publican, on the other hand, saw himself clearly; as did the thief that was crucified next to Jesus.

> *"And the publican, standing afar off, would not lift up so much as [his] eyes unto heaven, but smote upon his breast, saying, God be merciful to me a sinner. I tell you, this man went down to his house justified [rather] than the other: for every one that exalteth himself shall be abased; and he that humbles himself shall be exalted."*

Luke 18:13-14

"But the other answering rebuked him, saying, Dost not thou fear God, seeing thou art in the same condemnation? And we indeed justly; for <u>we receive the due reward of our deeds</u>: but this man hath done nothing amiss. And he said unto Jesus, Lord, remember me when thou comets into thy kingdom. And Jesus said unto him, Verily I say unto thee, To day shalt thou be with me in paradise."

Luke 23:40-**43**

These two had *selfless* attitudes. This is what God is seeking. The publican left the temple and went home justified before God and the thief went directly to heaven that very day. The selfless attitude will cause you to give of yourself in recognition of truth and justice. A selfless person will ignore their own needs at the cost of being uncomfortable and/or hurting themselves. It will cause you to do right in the face of death. They will endure embarrassment and humility in the face of others and withstand ridicule to achieve God's purpose.

The selfless attitude is a true giving, humble spirit. It is not easy and the enemy will want you to question yourself. The enemy will water that selfish seed to see if he can nurture it to grow in your spirit. He will ask, "Why should you?" He will tell you that others aren't or wouldn't. He will coax pride to rise up and dissuade you from moving in the right direction. We should be very simple in our response to ourselves – WWJD ("What Would Jesus Do?") When we can identify the response to this question, then we will be on the same track as the publican and the thief. We will then have the favor and blessings of God.

We really must be careful when Satan tries to download this program into our *hard drive*. This program will continually pull us away from God and turn us against everyone and everyone against us. Our lifestyle becomes a lifestyle that is focused solely on our own desires and on our own purpose. It will turn us against God as it did the first thief on the cross next to Jesus and cause us to put ourselves in God's place like the Pharisee.

If we read in the scriptures that God's commandment is that we are not to have any other God's before Him, this includes ourselves. Look at how God's wrath dealt with the gods of the Egyptians and the gods that the nations around Israel worshiped. Remember Sodom and Gomorrah and how God dealt with any sin that man committed that pulled him away from his creator.

The selfish attitude is dangerous because it incorporates all three of the categories that every sin can fall into. It consists of the lust of the eye; the lust of the flesh; _and_ the pride of life at the same time. The selfish person will see what hey want, calculate that it will make them or their flesh happy and become prideful to the point of obtaining their desire. If we can recognize this, then we must also recognize that this is not God or His mentality.

Being selfish has its reward just like every other endeavor that we undertake in life. Some people get their rewards on earth, but everyone will receive a reward when they get to heaven. It really boils down to which reward line you happen to be standing in. You will find that if you get into the selfish line in heaven, you will eventually receive your eternal reward from God when you move forward in line toward the 'White Throne'. That would be the, *"This is what I want" line."*

> *"And I saw a great white throne, and him that sat on it, from whose face the earth and the heaven fled away; and there was found no place for them."*

Revelation 20:11

Notes And Reflections For The Reader:

Notes And Reflections For The Reader:

History

I Am The Story

If I was the only man that God created and Satan desired to interfere with God's purpose for my life, He would have still sent Jesus. That is a humbling thought! It is all ***God's*** story, but He has chosen to make me a part of it. This is GOD; the creator of the entire universe from the biggest thing that we can see to the smallest thing that we cannot see.

The one scripture that has moved me and allowed me to hold onto my faith like no other is:

> *"Who shall separate us from the love of Christ? [shall] tribulation, or distress, or persecution, or famine, or nakedness, or peril, or sword? As it is written, For thy sake we are killed all the day long; we are accounted as sheep for the slaughter. Nay, in all these things we are more than conquerors through him that loved us. For I am <u>persuaded</u>, that neither death, nor life, nor angels, nor principalities, nor powers, nor things present, nor things to come, Nor height, nor depth, nor any other creature, shall be able to separate us from the love of God, which is in Christ Jesus our Lord."*

Romans 8:35-39

My aunt Ora-Lee in North Carolina simplified how to get from point A to point B in one very short sentence. When asked, *"How did you stay married for so long?"* she simply replied, ***"You have to make up your mind!"*** Now how simple is that? It answers the question directly and places the ball squarely back in your court. It is like anything else in life; it is *your* decision that *you* determine and live with. Being *persuaded* is the same thing.

Persuasion means:

persuade [per-Swede] verb (used with object), -persuaded, -dissuading.

1. to prevail on (a person) to do something, as by advising or urging: We could not persuade him to wait.

2. to induce to believe by appealing to reason or understanding; convince: to persuade the judge of the prisoner's innocence.

Origin:
1505–15; < Latin persuader. See per-, dissuade, suasion

Synonyms

1. urge, influence, move, entice, or impel. Persuade, induce imply influencing someone's thoughts or actions. They are used today mainly in the sense of winning over a person to a certain course of action: It was I who persuaded him to call a doctor. I induced him to do it. They differ in that <u>persuade suggests appealing more to the reason and understanding</u>: I persuaded him to go back to his wife (although it is often lightly used: Can't I persuade you to stay to supper?); induce emphasizes only the idea of successful influence, whether achieved by argument or by promise of reward: What can I say that will induce you to stay at your job? Owing to this idea of compensation, induce may be used in reference to the influence of factors as well as of persons: The prospect of a raise in salary was what induced him to stay.

For the most part, *however* you come to be persuaded, it is still a question of setting a determined course of action or of setting a direction for yourself, in your own mind. To be persuaded means that you have accepted a <u>belief</u> or a way of thinking.

After getting to this portion of my life and seeing how God has watched over me; blessed me; kept and encouraged me; supplied all of my needs and been faithful and loyal when I was not; I am **PERSUADED**! I have not been convinced or swayed by any particular person or forced in any way to believe or hold the convictions that I have. I am persuaded because I have found the truth. I have studied, compared and labored over which choices to make and found that Jesus is the **only** way. I could no longer believe that the way I was living would get me any place positive. A person always knows if they are living up to God's smallest expectations or even their own. It is inherent in us because we are designed this way. Above anything else, I knew myself and I *owned* it!

After we come to the end of ourselves and recognize that our way is not working anymore, we have to be honest with ourselves and decide to make a change. Either we fall into self deception or we stop and make a 180^0 turn. Self deception is dangerous, but repentance is what will get God's attention. When my mind was made up, God took the next step. Now I had hold of something that was real and that I could sink my teeth into. I began to ask God to show me His Word more deeply and I studied it in a way that led me to dig deeper still.

I have to say that I love Paul especially because he was so ingrained in and compassionate about his belief that he excelled beyond many that were his seniors. When Paul was persuaded, he placed as much enthusiasm and zeal into his changed mindset as he did with his former. He became a man who contributed 70% to the New Testament and won countless souls to Christ where he once killed those who followed Jesus. What Paul suffered for his faith is incredible, but the above scripture sums it up. Not dying or living or spiritual things or carnal things could dissuade him from what he believed. Nothing in the past and nothing in the future or anyone that would tell him anything against Jesus could change his mind. He viewed anything standing in his way as an obstacle that was trying to separate him from God's love through His son. This is an amazingly profound statement in and of itself, but what did Paul suffer in following his faith? Besides Paul's proclamation about being persuaded, Paul suffered for what he believed.

"*As the truth of Christ is in me, no man shall stop me* of this boasting in the regions of Achaean.

Paul found the truth and was adamant about no one being able to stop him from telling everyone about it. This truth was taking him around the world and into unknown territory.

> *Wherefore? because I love you not? God knoweth. But what I do, that I will do, that I may cut off occasion from them which desire occasion; that <u>wherein they glory, they may be found even as we</u>.*

He tells the church in Rome that he loves them and that he is going to stop anyone that is attempting to hinder Jesus' message of the 'Kingdom'. If anyone is in the same position that he was in (as Saul the persecutor of the church of Christ); anyone in the position of being prideful, Paul was going to erase that pride and place everyone on the same level playing field.

> *For such [are] false apostles, deceitful workers, transforming themselves into the apostles of Christ. And no marvel; for Satan himself is transformed into an angel of light. Therefore [it is] no great thing if his ministers also be transformed as the ministers of righteousness; whose end shall be according to their works.*

He plainly sees this as a trick of Satan and points out the enemy's plan. Paul's comparison is to Satan's army appearing as angels of light. Those that are on Satan's side will show themselves in a way that is seductive, tempting and seemingly accommodating to the present need or desire. Paul forces them to think by stating hat it is nothing special if Satan can use men who seem to be righteous to accomplish his deception.

> *I say again, Let no man think me a fool; if otherwise, yet as a fool receive me, that I may boast myself a little. That which I speak, I speak [it] not after the Lord, but as it were foolishly, in this confidence of boasting. Seeing that many glory after the flesh, I will glory also. For ye suffer fools gladly, seeing ye [yourselves] are wise. For ye suffer, if a man bring you into bondage, if a man devour [you], if a*

man take [of you], if a man exalt himself, if a man smite you on the face. I speak as concerning reproach, as though we had been weak. Howbeit wherein soever any is bold, (I speak foolishly,) I am bold also.

Paul then begins to be very bold toward the church in Rome. He begins to pull the foundation out from under those that believe themselves to be very high and mighty. He says that they can think what they want of him, but he asks them to look at themselves and make the comparison. This is a challenge that *persuaded* them! He is telling that he was once like them and he knows wherein their pride is based. What he is saying is that if he can do a 180⁰ and be convinced to this degree, then they surely can seeing that his former position was greater than theirs. He uses himself as an example by pointing out that the things that he has been persuaded of have made him bolder than he once was. He attempts to show them that his change of heart has its pros and cons, but is ultimately worth it.

Are they Hebrews? so [am] I. Are they Israelites? so [am] I. Are they the seed of Abraham? so [am] I. Are they ministers of Christ? (I speak as a fool) I [am] more;

He knows that he is speaking to learned men. He is not trying to take anything from them, but is attempting to add something to them, but he is, however being slightly sarcastic.

in labors more abundant, in stripes above measure, in prisons more frequent, in deaths oft. Of the Jews five times received I forty [stripes] save one. Thrice was I beaten with rods, once was I stoned, thrice I suffered shipwreck, a night and a day I have been in the deep; [In] journeying often, [in] perils of waters, [in] perils of robbers, [in] perils by [mine own] countrymen, [in] perils by the heathen, [in] perils in the city, [in] perils in the wilderness, [in] perils in the sea, [in] perils among false brethren; In weariness and painfulness, in watching often, in hunger and thirst, in fastings often, in cold and nakedness.

This portion is Paul's resume of suffering. He spells out that he has done more for his new cause than anyone else. He lists that he has more scars than he can count and that he has been in prison and in danger of death more often. He states that he has been beaten 199 times and beaten with rods on three separate occasions. He was stoned and in three different boat wrecks where on one he had to to tread water for a night and a day. In his travels, he has had to face thieves and strangers and has been in danger by his own countrymen as well. Paul says that he has faced danger in the country and in the city; on dry land and at sea. He has been among people who are not who they say they are and is constantly having to look over his shoulder. Even when he is cold naked and hungry; even when he is fasting, in pain, or naked he is focused on what he believes.

Something has made an impression on Paul and is driving him to face the dangers of the world to tell others. There is no doubt that Paul suffered all of these things externally and yet he also suffered internally in his body. His greatest concern was the proclamation of the gospel message and insuring that those who had already been persuaded were encouraged to hold on to their faith.

> *Beside those things that are without, that which cometh upon me daily, the care of all the churches."*

> 2 Corinthians 11:10-**28**

There are very few people that have been so convinced of their cause that they are willing to suffer all of these dangers and wrongs to establish and share their conviction. The list of these certain types of people would be very short and amongst the greatest men and women in human history. These people did not see themselves as special or extraordinary; they simply believed what they believed with an unsurpassed conviction.

Where will you find yourself in the chronicles of history? Will the things that you have fought for in this life carry on into eternity? When the world looks back at your record and life, will they remember that there was something of which you were persuaded? Will they be able to say that your story was the same as Hi Story?

Notes And Reflections For The Reader:

Notes And Reflections For The Reader:

Through Brian's Eyes

If we all saw the world through his eyes...

Brian is a friend of mine!

I remember when he was born. He's 13 years old now and he's autistic. Brian is <u>amazing</u>! Like most people that have autism, there are certain characteristics that they possess that the average person does not. They simply see the world differently than we do and therefore must express the world, in the way in which *they* perceive reality; in their **<u>own</u>** way.

The amazing thing about Brian is that he is incapable of anger. Digest *that* for a moment and think of everything that is associated with anger; and then remove it from the equation. I have seen Brian frustrated, I have seen Brian disappointed and I have even seen Brian discouraged, but most of these emotions are forced upon him by the people around him and not of his own design. These emotions may be confused as anger, but that is because, for the most part, we are too busy to actually pay true attention to what the issue may be; too busy to describe Brian's emotion correctly. They are merely reactions to what *he* is able to recognize as not being right, from his perspective. I have never seen him mad, angry, annoyed, aggravated, or upset. He simply does not possess these emotions or is not able to express them in a manner that we can recognize.

Anger in someone without autism, is usually expressed in words; communicated through facial expressions, played out through actions and shown in reprisal, retaliation and revenge. Neither of these things has ever been expressed in Brian'; as much as I have been in his presence so much as frowned; never. Things, that should have sent Brian over the edge, are dealt with in a fashion that would put us in remembrance of 'innocence lost'. There is something that is unsoiled by the world that exists in Brian; something pure! I have heard from others, for which Brian has done things, that would contradict the picture that I am painting here, but when I reflect on those things, I realize that Brian's greatest connection with our world is imitation. He imitates what he comes into the most frequent contact with. If what he comes into contact with is negative, then he mirrors that as best he can; it is his way of connecting. If what he comes into contact with is positive, then he mirrors that. He's not a robot and he *does* have a <u>very</u> distinct personality. The key to Brian is that *we* are the ones that need to be paying attention and not the other way around. I wish that I could say, "alright *then*" when I don't get *my* way and let that be that. I would be better than most if I didn't let my disappointments in life weigh me down and burden me. How many of us can dismiss the things in life that cause us the most pain and then are able to turn our attention to the very simplest of answers; change our focus? I've watched him take the very worst situation on the chin, express it in a fashion that seemed too simple for words and simply change his focus. Once Brian's focus is changed, there is no more problem for Brian. Again I will use this scripture…

> *Take therefore no thought for the morrow: for the morrow shall take thought for the things of itself. Sufficient unto the day [is] the evil thereof.*

> Matthew 6:34

How is it that Brian has mastered these three scriptures without having been taught or reading the word of God? The first three gospels hold the key:

> *But Jesus said, Suffer little children, and forbid them not, to come unto me: <u>for of such is the kingdom of heaven.</u>*

> Matthew 19:14

But when Jesus saw [it], he was much displeased, and said unto them, "Suffer the little children to come unto me, and forbid them not: <u>for of such is the kingdom of God.</u>"

Mark 10:14

But Jesus called them [unto him], and said, "Suffer little children to come unto me, and forbid them not: <u>for of such is the kingdom of God.</u>"

Luke 18:16

I am no doctor, but I do realize this; Brian's intelligence will grow as he grows and matures and learns more about himself and his surroundings. What I do not believe will change during the course of his lifetime is that loss of innocence. It is that childlike innocence that makes Brian so special even though at thirteen years old he's the size of a 6ft. man and weighs about 225lbs.

It's what we lose as the world begins to win and mankind's effects of eating from 'The Tree of the Knowledge of Good and Evil' begin to take root in our lives. We are all born into sin as a result of Adam giving up his birthright in Eden. There is however a reminder of that innocence, that we were originally intended to carry for eternity, still contained in us as children. This is what Brian has and it is what makes him *special, **not*** the autism.

Brian has the ability to see things from a child's perspective that is much younger than him. As he grows to manhood, his body will grow and change; he will learn more and more; he will be exposed to more and more negative influences and he will imitate some of these, as he struggles to identify with the world he lives in and his surroundings. Brian will not have the ability to merge and decipher, the way that we do, Each incident that we experience, perform or preform opinions about people. He, of course, has a self preservation response, but it does not extend toward selfishness or self-righteousness. His ideas about one person will never be based on his experience with another. Brian will always judge everyone for what *he* is able to remember about that particular person and never per-judge anyone. He will never say, *"You're just like him or just like her."* He will never compare <u>people</u> to other people, but will value each person for what they **contribute** or **remove** from his life.

I am proud to say that I have had the pleasure to see pictures of Brian skiing. Yes, skiing. It totally blew my mind and made me think, *"What can't Brian do?"*

Brian does not have the imagination to lie...Now *that* alone is special all by itself!

That is another thing that makes Brian beautiful!

I wish I saw things through Brian's eyes!

Thanks:

*These books on Spiritual Warfare would
not have been possible without:*
Nicole Marie Osborne-James (Lucianna-
The Don's wife aka Carmella)

Family:

Tammy Lynette James (Chica), Tamara Alicia James (Goose), Monique
Elizabeth James (Jigga), Dorian Briquet Lawson James (The Lousy
Kid), Nelijah Rene James (Little Moccasin), Judah Jamal Justice
James (Miho-Chico-Ese-Gringo), Israel Jordan James (Do), Pastor
Huston Robinson (Father), Minister Sherman Robinson (Mother),
Eloise Williams (Grandmother), Leonard Williams (Uncle), Pierre
& Yvonne Moody (Uncle & Aunt), Kathleen, Keisha & Anthony
Walker, Derrick (Big Brother) & Tracey (Sister – T-Bird) Hayes,
Pastor Lowell Tyrone (TY) Hawkins, Andre (Bink) Raymond Brown
& Lila (LaLa) Robinson, Patricia Brown, The Remnant & Zion.

Special Thanks (Friends & Extended Family)

<u>Bishop Etta Stephens - Banks</u> (Mom2) & The New Vision For Life
Church Family, Pastor Clyde G. Johnson, Pastor Carl Robinson &
Family, Minion, Philip, Ronnie, Philip Jr., & Gregory Lumpkin,
Hope Spry & Sterling Bethea, Noel K. Adkins, Sabrina Lake, Sierra,
Jasmine Lucas, Leonard & Tiffany Brown, Raymond Lewis & Family,
Crystal & Yvette Fox & Family, Crystal Edwards & Family, Minister
Bertha, Greg, & Roland Smith, Deacon Todd Cook & Family, May
Lawson & Family, Minister Steve Reynolds, 1st Lady Reynolds, &
Steve Jr., Thomas & Desiree Farr & Family, Gina Mulroney & Family,
Ivan, Toika & Vookie Makell, Frederick Hudson & Family, James &
Sandra Smith & Family, Kevin, Cameron, April Parks & Family,
Tamra & Frederic Cross, Jeff & Essie Lawson & Family, Capri &
Jasmine Cruz, Vanessa Warrick-Thornton & Harold Thornton III
(Ice), Jerome Jackson & Family, Patrick Ford & Family, Dillard Jones
& Family, Anselmo A. Gordon & Family, Brian D. Nichols, Phi Beta

Sigma Fraternity Inc., VERTIGO, Harold Robinson, Mark Brown & First Lady Olajuwon Hawkins. All of my Dear Readers and all of my past clients, everyone that has supported and pressed with me *with* and *without* knowing it!

Associates:

Darryl Nathaniel Hudson & Family, Byron James & Family, Pastor Nolan Leroy Henson & Pastor Terry Henson & Family, Pastor Linwood R. Taylor & First Lady Lillian Taylor, Wilbur Lucas, Associate Pastor Leroy Thomas, Barbara-Jean & Margo Ellis, Marcus & Mari McCoy, David, Charlene, Omega, Sheila, Dymon, & Brian Butler, Uncle Tim & Aunt Georgia Peay, Lillian, Frenchetta, Emmanuel & Christopher Smith, Laquanna, Claudia & Brittany Coupling, Kevin & Jacques Coupling, Latisha Scott & Family, Ronald Klein Man, Uzi Sellouk & Family, Michelle Mosley, Travisha Brown - Spruill & Family, Katrina Anderson, Yolanda Jackson, Roxanne White & Family, Sharon and Curtis Brown & Family, Eric & Lethargy Mitchell & Family, Mildred Arminger, Lawrence Lewis, Clifton Dorsey, India Brown, The Duguid Family.

MARANATHA